DISCONNECTED

Understanding Alzheimer's Disease

Connie Goldsmith

TFCB

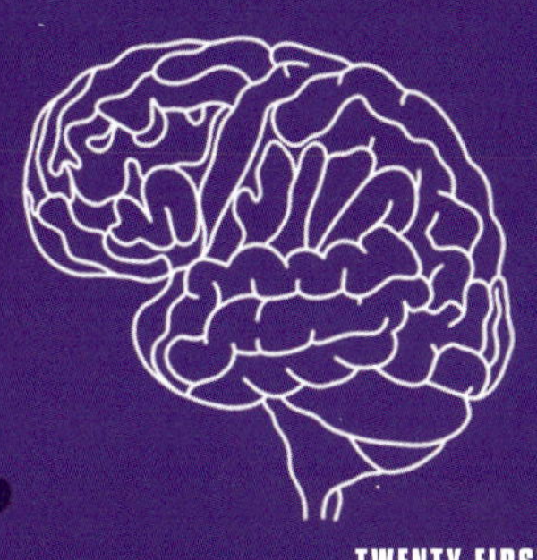

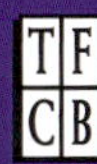

TWENTY-FIRST CENTURY BOOKS / MINNEAPOLIS

Dedicated to the families who love and care for people with Alzheimer's disease

Twenty-First Century Books™
An imprint of Lerner Publishing Group, Inc.
241 First Avenue North
Minneapolis, MN 55401 USA

For reading levels and more information, look up this title at www.lernerbooks.com.

Main body text set in Adobe Garamond Pro.
Typeface provided by Adobe Systems.

Library of Congress Cataloging-in-Publication Data

Names: Goldsmith, Connie, 1945– author.
Title: Disconnected : understanding Alzheimer's disease / Connie Goldsmith.
Description: Minneapolis : Twenty-First Century Books, [2025] | Includes bibliographical references and index. | Audience: Ages 11–18 | Audience: Grades 7–9 | Summary: "Alzheimer's disease is a dementia that affects the memory, thinking, and behavior of millions of Americans. Understand more about what Alzheimer's is through a look at its stages, current clinical research, caregiver accounts, and more" —Provided by publisher.
Identifiers: LCCN 2024016795 (print) | LCCN 2024016796 (ebook) | ISBN 9798765627594 (library binding) | ISBN 9798765659434 (epub)
Subjects: LCSH: Alzheimer's disease—Juvenile literature.
Classification: LCC RC523.3 .G65 2025 (print) | LCC RC523.3 (ebook) | DDC 616.8/311—dc23/eng/20240621

LC record available at https://lccn.loc.gov/2024016795
LC ebook record available at https://lccn.loc.gov/2024016796

Manufactured in the United States of America
1-1010945-52139-8/1/2024

Table of Contents

CHAPTER 1

Getting to Know Dementia

Our vision: A world without Alzheimer's and all other dementia.
—Alzheimer's Association, 2023

Past generations didn't usually talk about their family health, especially about certain stigmatized conditions such as dementia. Yet former teacher Maralyn Soifer will always remember when her grandmother changed.

> My parents both worked long hours, so I spent much of my time with my grandmother when I was in elementary school. She lived upstairs, and I lived downstairs with my parents. Grandma and I loved baking and cooking together. She used to walk me to school in the morning and home in the afternoon.

Grandma was my guardian angel until I was about nine or ten years old. Then all of a sudden, she changed drastically. She didn't walk me to school anymore, and I couldn't understand why she had to stay home all the time. She no longer baked or cooked. She didn't talk very much, not even to me. She just sat around. But no one told me why.

Grandma couldn't be alone, so my family hired a woman to help her. I asked my mom why the woman was upstairs with Grandma every day. Mom said she was there to help Grandma eat, get dressed, and to be sure she took her medicine. When I asked why Grandma needed help like that, my parents didn't give me much of an answer. They didn't tell me why she was sick. I didn't understand why Grandma was so quiet and lost in her own world. I spent many hours after school just sitting with her, even though she often forgot my name. I wanted it to last forever. But nothing lasts forever.

Grandma went into the hospital one New Year's Eve and never came home. I was twelve years old then and still didn't know what had happened. But I did realize that she was gone forever. Even though I asked my parents what was happening over and over again, they never told me anything. Now I realize that Grandma probably had some sort of dementia. She's gone, but I'll never forget her. She'll always be part of my life.

What Is Dementia?

Dementia is an umbrella term used to describe a collection of symptoms caused by various diseases. These symptoms result from abnormal brain changes and include a decline in an individual's cognitive abilities, such

Types of Dementia

Alzheimer's disease
60–80 percent

Lewy body dementia (DLB)
5 percent

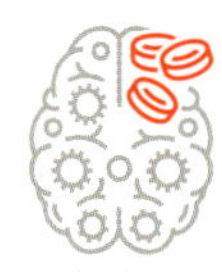

vascular dementia
5–10 percent

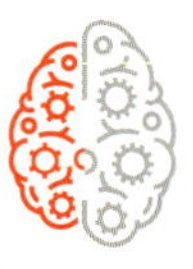

frontotemporal dementia (FTD)
10–20 percent

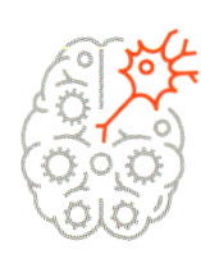

other

Alzheimer's disease is the most common type of dementia and makes up 60 to 80 percent of all dementia cases. It is followed by FTD, DLB, and vascular dementia. Other less common types include dementia caused by Huntingon's disease and mixed dementia.

as reasoning, thinking, and memory. While people with dementia can often remember events from the distant past, they are likely to have problems with short-term memory. For example, they may forget things that happened that morning or earlier that week. They may lose their purses or wallets, and they may forget to pay their bills. Dementia affects a person's ability to shop, prepare meals, keep appointments, and recognize family members, friends, and once-familiar places. These changes are severe enough to affect daily life, independent function, behavior, feelings, and relationships.

Dementia is *not* a normal part of aging. Older people might occasionally forget things, such as a common word, where they left their keys, and the name of an acquaintance they rarely see—but they usually recall these things later. Some people call these "senior moments," but they are seldom signs of dementia.

Meet Your Brain

A healthy brain works like a supercomputer. It stores things that you learn. It controls everything you say and do. It processes information that it receives from your body and all your senses. Your brain regulates breathing to make sure your body has enough oxygen. It also tells you when it's time to sleep because your body is tired.

Just like a computer, messages fly inside your brain at incredible speeds. For example, say you slam your finger in a drawer. The sensation of pain in your finger instantly reaches your brain. Your brain says, "Ouch! That hurts a lot." That message then goes to the part of your brain that tells your body what to do about the pain. It says, "Open the drawer and pull your finger out!" People also use their brain to think and solve problems. You use your brain to find answers for a math test, follow directions, and learn a new game.

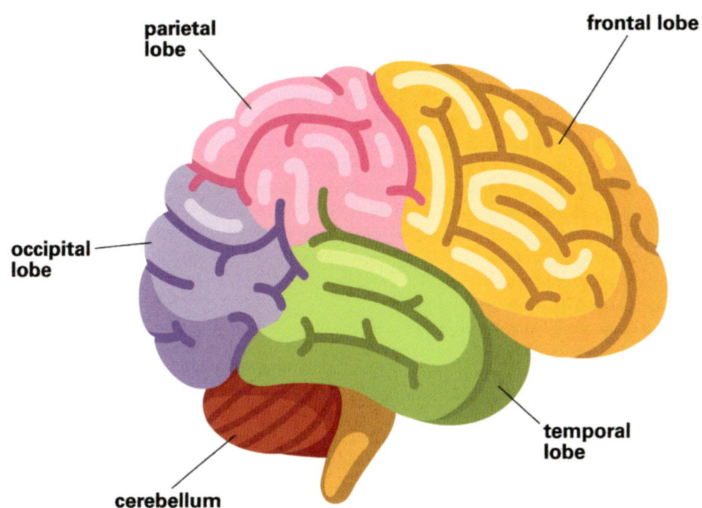

Different parts of the brain are affected by different types of dementia.

But unlike a computer, people experience emotions with their brain and then react to them. You hang out with your friends. That makes you happy. Your grade on the big history test isn't as good as you had hoped. That can make you both angry and sad. Your car gets a flat tire at night on an unfamiliar road. That might make you a little afraid. Our brains are the root of human intelligence and emotion, and all the parts work together to help us function. When these parts aren't functioning correctly, symptoms associated with dementia begin to occur. To understand why, let's take a look at the human brain.

Your brain is made up of distinct parts, called lobes:

- **The frontal lobe** is at the front of the brain. It's involved in personality, decision-making, movement, speech, and learning and recalling information.
- **The parietal lobe** is the middle part of the brain and helps you identify objects and understand spatial relationships—or knowing where your body is compared with objects around you. This lobe also helps you interpret pain and touch. Like the frontal lobe, the parietal lobe helps the brain understand spoken words.
- **The occipital lobe** is at the back of the brain and controls your vision.
- **The temporal lobe** helps with short-term memory, speech, processing sensory information, and recognizing odors. The temporal lobe has two parts, one on each side of the brain, behind your ears.
- **The cerebellum** lies beneath the occipital lobe. It helps control body movements, including balance and posture.
- **The cerebral cortex** is the outer layer of the brain. It is responsible for higher-level processes, including speech, memory, thinking, learning, and emotion.

Dementia affects different lobes. Its first symptoms are often problems with short-term memory. As dementia advances, it spreads and affects more parts of the brain, and can result in changed behavior and the loss of language and reasoning skills.

Types of Dementia

Scientists believe changes in the brain can begin twenty years or more before people actually begin to show symptoms of dementia. Dementia signals that something is going wrong. Many illnesses can cause dementia-like symptoms. Some of them are reversible, such as symptoms caused by depression, side effects of certain medications, drug or alcohol use, brain tumors, infections, and even a vitamin B-12 deficiency. In these cases, doctors can treat the underlying condition, and that often cures the symptoms.

But some types of dementia are irreversible, and they get worse over time. The four most common forms of irreversible dementia are Alzheimer's disease, frontotemporal dementia, Lewy body dementia, and vascular dementia. Dementias may have different causes, but what they have in common is the destruction and death of nerve cells in the brain.

Dementia Defined

The World Health Organization defines *dementia* as "a syndrome that can be caused by a number of diseases which over time destroy nerve cells and damage the brain, typically leading to deterioration in cognitive function (i.e., the ability to process thought) beyond what might be expected from the usual consequences of biological ageing."

ALZHEIMER'S DISEASE

Alzheimer's disease (AD) causes between 60 and 80 percent of dementia cases, making it by far the most common cause of dementia. Normally, our bodies make and use proteins to keep all our organs working correctly. But sometimes, two kinds of proteins—amyloid and tau—

Alzheimer's Association

The Alzheimer's Association is an organization that aims to eliminate Alzheimer's disease through research, provide and enhance care for all affected people, and reduce the risk of dementia through the promotion of brain health.

break into fragments inside the brain, forming what researchers call plaques and tangles. Plaques are deposits of damaged amyloid proteins that clump together and build up between brain cells. They prevent nerve cells from communicating with one another. Tangles are twisted fibers of tau proteins that gather inside brain cells that help transport nutrients to parts of the brain. Plaques and tangles in the brain are always present with Alzheimer's and visible after death during an autopsy. Both accumulate in areas of the brain that control memory and cognitive functions such as thinking, reasoning, problem-solving, and decision-making. Alzheimer's symptoms typically begin later in life, usually around the mid-sixties or later.

Early-onset Alzheimer's disease differs from the usual form of Alzheimer's. It can happen to people in their forties, fifties, and early sixties. Less often it can occur in people in their twenties or thirties. Usually, people with early-onset Alzheimer's disease carry one of the genetic mutations that predict the probability of getting it. Only 5 to 6 percent of Alzheimer's cases are early-onset Alzheimer's disease.

FRONTOTEMPORAL DEMENTIA

Frontotemporal dementia (FTD) causes between 10 and 20 percent of dementia cases. With FTD, nerve cells in the frontal and temporal lobes of the brain are damaged, causing dramatic changes in personality. People may become socially inappropriate, impulsive, and indifferent. Some people have trouble walking or lose the ability to speak normally. FTD tends to begin earlier than Alzheimer's, often starting between the ages of forty and sixty-five. Researchers are studying the genetic changes that seem to cause most cases of FTD.

KEVAN'S STORY: My Wife Had Alzheimer's Disease

Kevan Atteberry, author and illustrator of children's picture books, said his wife, Teri, was diagnosed with early-onset Alzheimer's disease when she was fifty-two.

A year before Teri's death, Kevan took her to a botanical garden where people were putting up Christmas lights. She moved slowly and couldn't form words, but her big smile told Kevan that she was having a good time.

It was ten days before our twenty-fifth wedding anniversary. This was after six months of testing, which she only agreed to after her family and friends kept suggesting that things were off and that she needed to find out why. Teri was in denial and would not participate in such conversations. She insisted everything was fine and her memory issues were just a part of menopause. We all knew different. And I know now she was aware of it too.

I found a couple of journals while sorting through her things after she died. Each had only one entry: a brief paragraph saying she was worried about her memory, and that friends and family were urging her to get tested. My guess is that she wrote in the first journal, forgot about it, and started another journal with a similar entry. Then forgot about that one too.

"I found a couple of journals while sorting through her things after she died. Each had only one entry: a brief paragraph saying she was worried about her memory, and that friends and family were urging her to get tested. My guess is that she wrote in the first journal, forgot about it, and started another journal with a similar entry. Then forgot about that one too."

—Kevan Atteberry

When we got the diagnosis, my family was stunned. We had never heard of early-onset Alzheimer's. Neither had anyone else, as we slowly let people know what was going on. Our two sons were shocked and heartbroken, but totally committed to give their mom their best. I did a deep dive into research about it and realized pretty quickly that the disease was a death sentence with absolutely no hope for treatment and no cure in sight.

It all played out as expected. She would get worse, eventually I'd have to place her in a facility, and then she would die. We discussed the future soberly, often with tears and a kind of hopeless resignation. But in the meantime, I wanted the best for her. And I channeled virtually everything into that. From then on, her care became my top priority. As the dementia took greater hold of Teri, we would switch up the caregiving, adding new

things she needed and letting go of things she didn't.

Both of our amazing sons stepped up. They were always there when I needed help or respite, as were other family members and friends. We were lucky to have many wonderful, caring souls in our lives. The eight and half years after her diagnosis went fast yet seemed to take a lifetime. I was able to give Teri full-time care until the last year and a half when it finally became too much for me.

The absolute hardest thing I ever had to do in my whole life was to place her in an adult family home.

An adult family home is a private home, which usually has three to five beds and a full-time staff to care for patients.

It took white lies and a lot of strength and support. She could sense things were changing. I visited her nearly every day, usually for lunch, and then took her for a walk. Her eyes would brighten when I got there. And even though she had lost the ability to form complete sentences a couple years earlier, I always knew what she was saying to me. At the beginning she would often ask me to take her home. I couldn't, of course, and it crushed me.

Eventually, she forgot about home. One small silver lining for Alzheimer's. Shortly after turning sixty-one, deep into dementia, she finished out her life the way she had lived her whole life, smiling.

Myths about Alzheimer's Disease

- Alzheimer's disease and dementia are the same thing.
- I will develop Alzheimer's disease if my parent has it.
- Only people in their seventies and older get Alzheimer's disease.
- Alzheimer's disease symptoms are normal as we get older.
- There are no treatments available for people with Alzheimer's disease.
- If I'm frequently forgetting things, it must be Alzheimer's disease.
- You can buy supplements online to prevent or cure Alzheimer's disease.
- You can prevent Alzheimer's disease.
- Doctors cannot definitively diagnose Alzheimer's disease until after death.
- An at-home genetic test can tell me if I have (or will have) Alzheimer's disease.
- I'm not a scientist. I can't do anything to help fight Alzheimer's disease.

LEWY BODY DEMENTIA

Lewy body dementia, specifically dementia with Lewy bodies (DLB), affects about 5 percent of dementia patients. Similar to Alzheimer's, DLB results from large deposits of an abnormal protein in the brain. Doctors call these deposits Lewy bodies. DLB tends to not only cause a decline in thinking and reasoning but also leads to visual and auditory hallucinations, sleep disorders, rigid muscles, and problems with movement.

VASCULAR DEMENTIA

Vascular dementia affects 5 to 10 percent of people with dementia. It occurs when blood flow to the brain decreases, such as during a stroke, which can cause blood clots that may block blood flow to the brain. In

Rachael Wonderlin: Dementia Care Consultant

Rachael Wonderlin is an internationally recognized dementia care consultant with a master's degree in gerontology, the study of aging. In 2014 she founded Dementia by Day, a dementia care consulting business. The organization offers support to care communities and senior living providers, as well as families and caregivers, on how to communicate with and manage dementia patients. She has written three books about dementia and caregiving, including *When Someone You Know Is Living in a Dementia Care Community: Words to Say and Things to Do*, all published by Johns Hopkins University Press.

some patients, vascular dementia develops gradually due to many tiny strokes and other conditions that affect blood flow in the brain. The reduced blood flow deprives the brain of oxygen and nutrients needed for normal brain function. Symptoms of vascular dementia depend on which parts of the brain are affected and can include the inability to pay attention, difficulty finding the right words, and uncontrollable laughing or crying.

ASSESSING ALZHEIMER'S

With all these forms of dementia, how do doctors know if a person has Alzheimer's or something else? Friends and family or household members can watch the person's behavior and take the person to their primary care doctor if something seems off. The doctor talks to the person and likely gives verbal and written tests to evaluate memory and thinking abilities. If it appears as if the person needs further evaluation, the doctor then refers the person to a specialist.

Until a few years ago, the only way to be certain that a person had Alzheimer's was to examine their brain tissue after death to see if the characteristic amyloid plaques and tau tangles were present. Today, specialized brain scans and blood tests can lead to an accurate diagnosis, which leads to earlier treatment.

MARGARITA'S STORY: My Mamá Has Alzheimer's Disease

Margarita Engle, award-winning Cuban American author and poet, said one of the hardest weeks of her life was when she had to move her mother, Eloisa, from a hospital into memory care.

> **For years, I had been trying to talk my parents into moving in with my husband and me, but they refused. After my father died, Mamá stopped paying bills and bathing. She hoarded junk mail, barely slept or ate, and still refused to move in with us. A doctor, social worker, and attorney all told me it was illegal to move her against her will, so I obtained power of attorney and took over her financial and medical decisions. I hired a part-time caregiver for her, but Mamá was still alone at night, two hundred miles [322 km] away from me.**

After Margarita's mother fell in her own house, she was briefly hospitalized. The fact that Eloisa had injured herself made it legal for Margarita to move her. By then, Eloisa's Alzheimer's was so severe that she needed twenty-four-hour care.

> **I realized that my mother might feel lost in a big, crowded memory care facility, so I chose a small boarding care home. It's an ordinary house owned by a nurse, with six residents and a live-in group of skilled caregivers as well as a night caregiver. On the day when the move was scheduled, my husband and I had COVID, so we had to hire medical transportation to take Mamá to the home. My son was there to greet his grandma when she arrived. The whole experience was traumatic, tragic, and frightening. Mamá was angry and confused. But I decided to focus on the positive outcome: at least she's safe now.**

Abby was bred to herd cattle but became an unofficial therapy dog for Margarita's mother, Eloisa, and the other memory care patients where Eloisa lives.

My husband and I visit Mamá every morning, and our son visits on the weekends. Our daughter and my sister live too far away to come often, but our border collie, Abby, loves to visit. Abby cuddles with Mamá and the other residents, even though she's not a trained service dog. Instinctively, Abby understands that people are comforted by the simple gift of companionship.

Mamá does word search puzzles, reads, and knits, but she's rapidly losing the ability to do those activities, along with her memory and language skills. Often, we just leaf through a magazine together, looking at pictures of flowers and birds. Abby always provides a subject for conversation. "She's a good dog," Mamá says over and over, looking pleased to have a best friend with soft fur and gentle expectations.

CHAPTER 2

All about Alzheimer's Disease

If I get dementia, don't exclude me from parties and family gatherings.
—Rachael Wonderlin, dementia consultant

How much do you know about Alzheimer's disease? Take this simple five-question true-false quiz on the next page to test your knowledge of Alzheimer's. Make your best guess, and then compare how many questions you get correct now with how many you get right after you finish this chapter. The answers may surprise you.

TRUE OR FALSE?

- Age is the best-known risk factor for Alzheimer's disease.
- High blood pressure may increase the risk for Alzheimer's disease.
- Family history does not play a role in developing Alzheimer's disease.
- Alzheimer's disease is one of the top ten leading causes of death in the United States.
- Alzheimer's disease is a normal part of aging.

Who Gets Alzheimer's?

While the chance of getting Alzheimer's varies between biological sex and among ethnic groups, age is by far the greatest risk factor for developing it. Scientists believe that after the age of sixty-five, the risk of developing Alzheimer's doubles about every five years. Younger people may get Alzheimer's disease, but it's much less common.

According to the Centers for Disease Control and Prevention (CDC), "Normal brain aging may mean slower processing speeds and more trouble multitasking. But routine memory, skills, and knowledge are stable and may even improve with age." Memory problems that interfere with a person's ability to do everyday tasks are often one of the first warning signs of Alzheimer's disease.

Although scientists are learning more about Alzheimer's every day, they still don't know the exact cause. While about one-third of people aged eighty-five and older may have Alzheimer's disease, many people live well into their nineties and beyond without ever developing it. Even so, scientists believe that normal age-related changes in the brain add to the damage that Alzheimer's causes. These changes can include shrinkage of certain parts of the brain, inflammation, damage to blood vessels, and breakdown of energy production within brain cells.

Alois Alzheimer

In 1906 German psychiatrist and neuroanatomist Alois Alzheimer spoke to a group of psychiatrists at a university in Munich, Germany. He had identified an unusual brain disease in Auguste Deter, one of his patients who had recently died at the age of fifty. Deter had developed paranoia, confusion, aggression, and problems with sleep and memory. When her situation worsened, she checked in to the psychiatric hospital where Alzheimer worked. He was her doctor for five years. But he could not identify how to treat her condition.

After Deter died, Alzheimer examined her brain and discovered what he called, "a peculiar severe disease process of the cerebral cortex." Damaged proteins in Deter's brain had formed plaques and tangles. He also noted that her cerebral cortex was thinner than a healthy person's. The findings excited Alzheimer's colleague, Dr. Emil Kraepelin, also a psychiatrist. But Alzheimer's presentation at the medical conference in Munich gained little attention.

Alois Alzheimer

Over the next few years, Alzheimer published other papers describing similar abnormalities in the brains of four more patients. In 1910 Kraepelin named the disease that Alzheimer had identified: Alzheimer's disease. Still, the larger medical world paid little attention to Alzheimer's findings. He died in 1915 without knowing that his name would one day become common around the world.

In 2016 researchers Rachel Whitmer (*left*), Elizabeth Rose Mayeda (*right*), and others released a fourteen-year study on Alzheimer's risk examining six racial and ethnic groups in Oakland, California. Their study found that Black and Native Americans had a much higher average annual rate of dementia incidences than Asian and white Americans.

In the US, women live about six years longer than men on average, so it's not surprising that more women than men have Alzheimer's. Nearly two-thirds of Americans with Alzheimer's are women. Women who reach the age of forty-five have a one-in-five chance of developing Alzheimer's as they age, while the risk is one in ten for men.

Age is not the only reason why so many more women than men develop Alzheimer's. Women have stronger immune systems than men do, and some researchers believe this may be one reason why women develop Alzheimer's more often. A 2018 Harvard study suggested that female bodies may deposit harmful plaque in the brain to help fight off infections.

Following advanced age, family history is the second-strongest risk factor for developing Alzheimer's disease. Studies of families and twins indicate that genetic factors play a role in at least 80 percent of Alzheimer's cases.

Race and ethnicity also influence who develops Alzheimer's. For example, Black Americans are about twice as likely as white Americans to develop Alzheimer's and other dementias. A study in 2020 showed

Percentage of Americans over Age Seventy with Alzheimer's Disease or Other Dementias, by Race

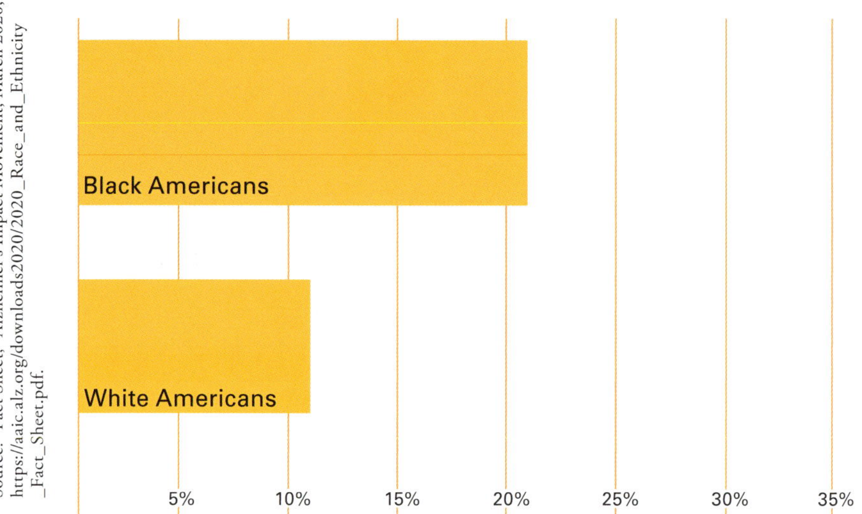

The percentage of Black Americans and white Americans aged seventy-one and older with Alzheimer's and other dementias in 2020

that 11 percent of white Americans and 21 percent of Black Americans aged seventy-one and older have Alzheimer's and other dementias. David Ajibade, MD, is a Nigerian educator who lives in Baltimore, Maryland, and works with the Alzheimer's Association. According to Ajibade, Black people are more likely to have vascular issues, problems related to sugar processing, resistance to insulin, and vitamin D deficiencies, which all impact brain health. Changing certain behaviors to manage these problems may lead to decreased cases of dementia. He says, "My main goal is to educate and help people see [that] what they're doing or not doing can be leading them towards a path of dementia. I thought it was important for us to understand [the reason behind these statistics] so that we could help people in impoverished communities or people who are most likely affected by it, especially African Americans."

Hispanic Americans are about one and a half times more likely than non-Hispanic white Americans to have Alzheimer's and other dementias.

According to the Alzheimer's Association, more than half of Hispanic Americans believe that losing memory and cognitive abilities is a normal part of aging, so they may be less likely to seek medical care. Learning about Alzheimer's is important and will help people recognize what is normal behavior and what may be a sign of Alzheimer's disease.

Although the rate of Alzheimer's and other dementias in Black Americans and Hispanic Americans is higher than in non-Hispanic white Americans, Black and Hispanic Americans are less likely to be diagnosed with the condition. And if diagnosed, it's often in the later stages, when they are more mentally and physically impaired. Due to social inequalities, Black Americans and Hispanic Americans are less likely to have health insurance, more likely to be low-income or live in low-income communities, and are more likely to receive inadequate medical care than non-Hispanic white Americans, often due to prejudice. In addition to those factors, high blood pressure and diabetes among marginalized communities can lead to higher rates of Alzheimer's. Management of these health conditions may lead to a lower risk of Alzheimer's disease.

Asian Americans are the fastest-growing racial and ethnic group in the United States. Compared to non-Hispanic white, Hispanic, and Black Americans, they are less likely to develop Alzheimer's, accounting for less than 10 percent of all Alzheimer's cases in the United States. But Asian Americans are underrepresented in studies of Alzheimer's, making up less than 3 percent of study participants. Could that low participation in studies skew the data?

The National Institute on Aging, part of the National Institutes of Health, is funding a study with sixteen academic research centers to look at Alzheimer's disease among Asian Americans and Asian Canadians. As of May 2023, nearly two thousand people had joined the study. Researchers plan to enroll five thousand people of Chinese, Korean, and Vietnamese ancestry in the study. Participants will fill out questionnaires, receive cognitive assessments, and provide saliva or blood samples for genetic testing.

PATTY'S STORY: My Sister Had Alzheimer's Disease

Patty Gregory's sister, Barbara Holman, lived with Alzheimer's disease for several years, and it greatly affected the family.

> **Words cannot convey the pain and adjustments people must go through when a loved one has Alzheimer's. It's like the de-evolution of a person's entire life. When Barbara was still alive, she lived at home with her husband, Roger. Olga, a recent Ukrainian immigrant, was our caregiving angel. She worked five hours a day during the week, and she was a dream for Barbara and our family. Olga was taking English classes, and before Barbara's Alzheimer's got really bad, the two of them would look at early vocabulary books together, with Barbara sounding out the English words and Olga repeating them. But one day, Barbara could no longer understand what they were doing.**

Barbara was in the hospital twice before her family put her on home hospice care. Hospice care focuses on helping patients who are nearing the end of their lives be more comfortable, sometimes taking them off certain medications or stopping treatment that causes discomfort. Home hospice care means the patient no longer visits the doctor or goes to the hospital. Instead, they remain at home with family members and receive at-home care.

During the months Barbara was on hospice, Patty, Roger, and Barbara's only daughter, Terra, were there every day. They did everything: helped nurses bathe Barbara, turned her so she wouldn't get bedsores, and changed her bed.

> **Barbara was never alone. I was with her from 11:00 am to 9:00 pm, while Roger covered nights. A temporary**

medical aide came on the weekends when Olga wasn't there. Terra or her husband would bring their children by every day after school. Barbara's grandson liked to push his grandmother around the house in her wheelchair.

Even though we fed Barbara three times a day she began to lose weight. I had hoped that she would come out of the downturn, but her body was slowing down along with her brain.

Barbara Holman (*right*) enjoys a special treat in Hawaii along with her daughter, Terra (*left*). At the time, Barbara's family noticed she was often forgetful, but she hadn't yet been diagnosed with Alzheimer's.

After being in hospice care for only a few months, Barbara died at home with her loved ones. "I'll always remember the smile she gave me the day before she died," Patty said.

Patty recommends that people who have a loved one with Alzheimer's disease contact their local Alzheimer's Association office. The organization offers classes for patients and their caregivers, and support groups for family members and friends. She would also like young people to know that if a loved one or family member gets Alzheimer's, it's nobody's fault.

"Your family is going through a very difficult time when this happens. Know that this is a natural event and there is no one to blame. Do what you can for them. Bring little bouquets of flowers. Talk to the person. You may think they don't understand, but they can hear you. Knowing that you are there makes them feel better. Remember, just being you is the greatest gift you can give to another person," she said.

Recognizing Alzheimer's around the World

September is World Alzheimer's Month. Since 2012 the goal of World Alzheimer's Month has been to increase public awareness of Alzheimer's disease and to give organizations around the globe the opportunity to reach out to the public. Alzheimer's disease is one of the biggest health crises of this century. As the world's aging population grows, the impact of Alzheimer's will continue to increase.

World Alzheimer's Month brings people together, especially those who are living with dementia, their families, caregivers, medical professionals, and scientists. Each year a theme is selected to educate people about dementia. For example, the theme for 2023 was "Never too early, never too late." It centered on risk factors for dementia and how to reduce them.

September 21 is World Alzheimer's Day. On this day, many organizations and associations around the world host memory walks, hold fundraisers, and promote campaigns to call attention to people affected by Alzheimer's disease and other kinds of dementia. Think about taking part in an activity that day to support families, friends, and neighbors who may be living with Alzheimer's disease.

In 2013 people in Texas took part in a butterfly release event, organized by the Alzheimer's Alliance. Participants donated twenty-five dollars for each butterfly they released. Proceeds from the event went toward helping Alzheimer's patients and caregivers in the local community.

Lifestyle Risk Factors

Age, biological sex, ethnicity, and genetics are all risk factors for developing Alzheimer's disease. They cannot be changed. But some lifestyle traits and medical conditions are also known to increase the chances for developing Alzheimer's disease. Here are some factors that put people at risk for developing Alzheimer's disease and other dementias, and what people can do about them:

- **Physical inactivity.** A lack of physical activity can increase the risk of developing Alzheimer's and other dementias. Adults should aim for about 150 minutes of moderate activity—such as brisk walking—each week to help promote their physical and brain health.
- **Type 2 diabetes.** Diabetes increases the risk of heart disease and stroke, which can damage the heart and blood vessels. Damaged blood vessels in the brain often contribute to cognitive decline. High blood sugar, which is present with diabetes, causes inflammation, which may damage brain cells. Managing diabetes reduces the risk of developing Alzheimer's as well as other medical conditions.
- **Smoking.** Smoking cigarettes greatly increases the risk for developing dementia. It also increases the risk for other diseases, including type 2 diabetes, stroke, heart disease, and several types of cancer. People who quit smoking, or are nonsmokers, decrease their chances of developing Alzheimer's later in life.
- **Alcohol consumption.** Excessive alcohol use increases the risk for dementia because alcohol can damage how the brain transmits signals between different regions. Drinking in moderation or not drinking at all lowers the risk for developing Alzheimer's.
- **Social contact.** Staying socially connected can lower one's risk for developing Alzheimer's. People who build

connections with others and stay socially active improve their brain health.

- **Obesity.** Obesity, especially during middle age (about ages forty to sixty), is linked to a higher risk of developing Alzheimer's. Regular exercise and eating a balanced diet can help decrease the risk.
- **Hypertension.** High blood pressure, especially during middle age, can increase a person's risk for Alzheimer's disease. It can also lead to heart disease and other health problems. Taking medication to control blood pressure is the only known treatment to help prevent Alzheimer's.
- **Depression.** Although depression is associated with Alzheimer's, and often occurs before a person is diagnosed with dementia, researchers are not sure if dementia causes depression or if depression cause dementia. Treating and managing depression is important to help people lead fulfilling lives.

In one study, researchers with the Chicago Health and Aging Project looked at how certain healthy behaviors can affect the risk of developing Alzheimer's disease. The healthy behaviors included the following: not smoking, regular exercise, light-to-moderate alcohol use, a balanced diet, and engaging in cognitive activities such as reading, writing, visiting a library, and playing games. Researchers followed these behaviors for seventeen years in over eighteen hundred individuals with an average age of seventy-three. They found that people who practiced four or five healthy behaviors had a 60 percent lower risk of developing Alzheimer's compared to those who practiced only one or no healthy behaviors. The association between practicing healthy behaviors and a lower risk for Alzheimer's was similar across biological sexes and across multiple ethnic groups.

MARK'S STORY: My Dad Has Alzheimer's

Mark Zanzinger's dad, Ron Zanzinger, has had Alzheimer's for several years.

> **At first, my mom and I began to notice changes in my dad's behavior. He kept repeating himself and forgetting what he was doing. He would say something completely off the wall like, "Look at the sun," when it was really the moon. He often said something mean-spirited about someone when he never had an unkind word to say about anyone before. My mom and sister had more of a grasp of what would be ahead than I did. At the time, I didn't know much about Alzheimer's. I knew it was a terrible disease, but I didn't quite understand how bad it would be. Seeing my dad decline week after week has been very hard to deal with. And the worst part is, there's really nothing you can do about it.**

Mark said it was tricky to learn how to best communicate with his dad. People with Alzheimer's often ask the same question over and over because they don't remember the answer. Mark realized it was easier for him to ask his dad a question than for his dad to ask him the same question several times. "You've got to be patient," Mark said. "That's all you can do."

Ron's family eventually moved him to a memory care facility. Mark noted that his dad seems to be doing well there.

> **He's made friends and they do activities together. I truly believe this helped him in some ways. When he lived at home with my mom, it was basically just the two of them. They hadn't been in that house for very long, so they didn't have many friends in the neighborhood yet. To be**

honest, I believe it accelerated his Alzheimer's because Mom and Dad didn't have much to do. At the new place—the memory care home—his decline slowed down a bit because he's mentally active every day.

People caring for loved ones with Alzheimer's often must deal with issues they never thought of before. For example, Mark had two surprises.

Something that I didn't see coming was how lonely my mom got when my dad went into memory care. It must be hard to deal with—living with your partner for many years and then one day he's gone. I've spent more time with my mom than with my dad lately because she seems to need me more. She's getting therapy now and that's helping. It's about an eighty-mile [130 km] round trip for me with heavy traffic from my house, but I see either Mom or Dad most weekends.

The second surprise Mark had was learning how he and his sister would split responsibilities.

When something this big happens, it's important to know who's in control. You'd think the spouse—my mom in this case—would be in control, but she couldn't manage it. Then it took several weeks for my sister and I to establish who was in control of what. Now we've got it mostly worked out. She's taking the full brunt of the financial part. She can afford it and I can't, so I'm okay with that. But I'm the one who goes nearly every Saturday to see my parents, even though I work full-time. That makes it tough. I don't think my sister fully realizes how difficult it

is. And if there's a sudden problem, I'm the one who gets a call and has to deal with it. My sister can only visit every three or four months. I hold no grudge against her because she has her own problems. But sometimes I get flustered with this role and I'm not always sure how to handle it.

Ron Zanzinger enjoying the fresh air on the patio of his memory care home

We've finally turned the tide, and my mom is in much better shape now and my sister and I are getting along better as well. The entire situation is a reality check. The sooner you can prepare yourself mentally and financially for something like this, the better off you'll be. You can team up with other family members and split the duties, so all the burden isn't on one person. It's a hard thing to do, and you've got to work at it. But remember, you're doing your loved one the final favor, and that should make you feel good.

"The entire situation is a reality check. The sooner you can prepare yourself mentally and financially for something like this, the better off you'll be."

—Mark Zanzinger

Alzheimer's by the Numbers

- About one-third of seniors die with Alzheimer's or another dementia.
- Alzheimer's is the seventh-leading cause of death in the United States.
- One in nine people who are sixty-five and over has Alzheimer's.
- Deaths from heart disease—the leading cause of death in Americans—are decreasing. But deaths from Alzheimer's are increasing, doubling between 2000 and 2019.
- Every three seconds a new case of Alzheimer's or dementia occurs somewhere in the world.

Knowing the Signs

Alzheimer's affects millions of families around the world. It can be a frightening disease, but the more that research uncovers about the disease, the better it can be managed and perhaps prevented in the future. People can learn to recognize the signs of the possible onset of Alzheimer's.

CHAPTER 3

Signs and Symptoms

If I get dementia, treat me the way that you would want to be treated.
—Rachael Wonderlin, dementia consultant

Changes in the brain can appear as early as twenty years before a person recognizes them as signs of Alzheimer's disease. When early symptoms do appear, some people don't realize that anything is wrong at first. They may deny having problems. Others may admit they're having problems doing certain things but believe it's just a sign of getting older. Although forgetting a few things occasionally may be a normal part of aging, it should not affect the ability to function in daily life.

"Most Alzheimer's dementia patients are not aware of their deficiency," Dr. Wessam Labib, a medical director at Loma Linda University Health, said. "Ignoring signs in your loved ones is the worst thing you can do for them. Flags can begin to be raised when we notice our loved ones are forgetting things they could manage before. But you must have a baseline and that will vary from person to person." For example, that baseline could include paying household bills on time. But perhaps a spouse took care of that in the past. So if a person isn't sure how to pay bills, that isn't necessarily a flag. But if a person who has been driving for decades starts to forget where they're going or how to stay in their own lane, that is a red flag.

Early Symptoms of Alzheimer's

A person can look for signs that someone they know is developing Alzheimer's disease or another form of dementia. According to the Alzheimer's Association, people with early signs of Alzheimer's disease (not to be confused with early-onset Alzheimer's) may experience these ten symptoms:

1. **Memory loss that disrupts daily life.** This is the most common early sign of Alzheimer's. It includes forgetting recently learned information, important dates and events, and asking the same questions over and over. *A typical age-related change is sometimes forgetting names or appointments but usually remembering them later.*
2. **Problems with planning or problem-solving.** People with signs of Alzheimer's may be unable to make and stick to a plan or be unable to solve a problem, such as following a familiar recipe or keeping track of monthly bills. They may also take more time to do things than before. *A typical age-related change is making occasional errors with finances or household bills.*
3. **Difficulty with completing familiar tasks.** This could include driving to a familiar location, keeping a grocery list, or remembering the rules of a favorite game such

as Scrabble or Monopoly. *A typical age-related change is occasionally asking for help using familiar technology or finding the best route to a new store across town.*

4. **Confusion with time or place.** People living with Alzheimer's may lose track of the year or season and not realize how much time is passing. They may forget where they are or how they got there. *A typical age-related change is forgetting the day of the week but figuring it out later.*
5. **Trouble understanding visual images and spatial relationships.** This can lead to problems with balance and reading. Problems with recognizing color, such as seeing a red light, and judging distance between cars can make driving hazardous. *A typical age-related change is developing cataracts or other medical problems with vision.*
6. **New problems with words when speaking or writing.** Some people with early Alzheimer's may have trouble beginning a conversation or participating in one. They may stop in the middle of saying something and then have no idea what they were going to say next. They may struggle with common words or use the wrong name. *A typical age-related change is occasionally forgetting the right word.*
7. **Misplacing things and being unable to retrace one's steps.** Someone living with Alzheimer's may put things in odd places. For example, they may put milk in a cupboard instead of the refrigerator. They may misplace things in the house and be unable to find them again. *A typical age-related change is misplacing things from time to time and usually being able to retrace one's steps to find them.*
8. **Changes in judgment and decision-making.** People with early signs of Alzheimer's may begin to make different decisions than they usually would make. For example,

Ten signs and symptoms of Alzheimer's disease

they might leave twenty dollars to pay for a soda that costs two dollars. Personal care and grooming may also decline in this stage. *A typical age-related change is occasionally miscounting money when paying for something.*

9. **Withdrawing from social activities.** A person with Alzheimer's may cut down on social activities or eliminate them entirely because they cannot follow conversations. They may have trouble keeping up with things they used to enjoy or are no longer interested in. *A typical age-related change is sometimes not being interested in family or social activities.*
10. **Changes in mood and personality.** As the disease progresses, people may become confused, suspicious, depressed, or anxious. They may become upset at home, with family, or with friends. *A typical age-related change is having a specific way of doing something and becoming upset if someone disrupts a familiar routine.*

Anyone who is experiencing these signs should see a doctor as soon as possible.

Stages of Alzheimer's Disease

Symptoms of Alzheimer's gradually worsen with time, and the patient's ability to function declines. Knowing what stage of Alzheimer's a person is in lets caregivers and providers know how to best help them. Of course, everyone is different, and stages can overlap, but in general, patients are classified as having mild, moderate, or severe Alzheimer's.

EARLY-STAGE ALZHEIMER'S (MILD)

In the early stage of Alzheimer's, people may still be able to function independently. They may drive, work, and take part in many social activities. A person in this stage may realize they're having memory lapses or forgetting familiar words. Family members and friends may notice something is not quite right. Common difficulties in early-stage Alzheimer's include not coming up with the right word or name, not remembering names after being introduced to new people, forgetting something they just read, losing or misplacing a valuable object, and increased difficulty with planning and organizing activities.

During the early stage of Alzheimer's, people developing dementia can still live a fulfilling life. They can focus their energy on the parts of their lives that are most important to them. At this time, people with early Alzheimer's and their family should put their legal, financial, and end-of-life plans in place while they are still able to.

MIDDLE-STAGE ALZHEIMER'S (MODERATE)

This is usually the longest stage, and it can last for many years. And as time goes on, people with Alzheimer's require more care. People in the middle stage of Alzheimer's are likely to confuse words; get angry, frustrated, or moody; or act in unexpected ways. Damage in the brain makes it difficult for them to express thoughts and perform even the most routine tasks, such as bathing or using the bathroom, without help or reminders.

The US Postal Service released this stamp in 2017. It shows a woman with Alzheimer's disease and a caregiver's hand resting on her shoulder. Most stamps at the time sold for forty-nine cents, but this special stamp sold for sixty cents. The US Postal Service donated the extra cost to fund research into Alzheimer's disease.

Symptoms in this stage can include forgetting events and personal history such as addresses and phone numbers, or the high school or college they attended. People may be confused about where they are or what day it is. They are likely to need help getting dressed. They may have problems sleeping and tend to wander and become lost. Their behavior often changes, including becoming suspicious, becoming impulsive, having delusions, and showing repetitive behaviors.

People living in the middle stage of Alzheimer's can continue to participate in some activities with help. Loved ones can figure out what the person is still able to do and can find a way to simplify tasks. At this time, the need for intensive care increases and caregivers may want to consider taking a break for themselves, such as putting their loved one in an adult day-care center, a nonresidential center with staff to look after the needs of older adults with dementia, for several hours a day, or hiring a person to help at home for a few afternoons a week.

MICHELE'S STORY: My Mom Had Alzheimer's

Michele Langhorst's mother, Annette Langhorst, had Alzheimer's disease.

My mom was sixty-three when my dad and my brother and I started to notice that she couldn't remember certain words or people's names that she'd known for years. She forgot questions we asked her and forgot where things were in the house and where she was going when she was driving. She couldn't figure out how to pick up a fork or how to use it correctly. This was out of character for her. She was always as sharp as a tack.

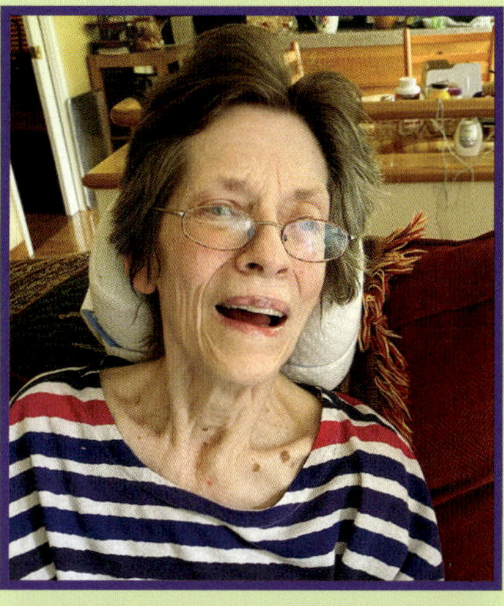

Annette used to smile when Michele visited her. During these visits, Annette did not recognize Michele and called her the kind lady who came to see her.

My grandmother had Alzheimer's disease, and we knew it was time to have Mom checked out to see if she also had it. My dad and I wanted to be prepared for what was going to happen next. I was especially sad because my mom and I were starting to have a closer relationship than we had before, but now that would never happen. Even though we all suspected that my mom would have Alzheimer's, it doesn't make it easier when you get the diagnosis. You keep telling yourself that maybe she won't get it like her mother did. You try to believe that so you can make it through the long journey ahead.

Genetic testing showed that Michele's mom had early-onset Alzheimer's disease—Alzheimer's that begins before the age of sixty-five. Following this, Michele and her brother were also tested for the gene that causes early-onset Alzheimer's. Both their tests were negative.

The hardest part of Alzheimer's was to watch my mom lose herself inside and out. It's like dealing with little deaths: the death of memory and the death of the time when she could walk and feed herself. I've watched her deteriorate into nothingness for several years. I've lost the person she was. She used to be someone who loved life and always looked her best. Now all I have are the memories that I cling to.

For a long time, Annette lived at home with live-in caregivers.

We first put Mom in a memory care facility. But she was so much younger than most of the other residents, the staff didn't pay enough attention to her. For example, she needed help with eating, but instead, the staff didn't make sure she got to her meals. Apparently, they assumed she would eat if she was hungry. Instead, they let her sleep whenever she wanted to. She ended up losing thirty pounds [14 kg] in three months! My dad and I decided that she really needed one-on-one care at home. The level of care that a person needs depends on the person. If they are responsive, they may do all right in a memory care facility. If not, then one-on-one care is the best outcome.

Michele's dad had a relationship with another woman, and they lived together in a separate house.

Mom would have wanted him to be happy and to get on with his life. His relationship never made me angry. Dad went back to work at age seventy to pay for Mom's care. Just because he lived somewhere else doesn't mean he stopped caring for or visiting Mom. They had been together since they were in the tenth grade! I once told him that I didn't want his heart to be broken in his new relationship, and he answered, "Your mom already broke my heart." Survivors need love too! I'm happy that my dad found love again.

Michele wants people to know a few things if they have a loved one with Alzheimer's.

Don't be upset when they no longer know who you are. It can be very hurtful when suddenly your parent or grandparent is not sure who you are. I remember my nephew came to visit my mom one summer. She wasn't sure who he was, and she was always getting mad at him. Her actions hurt and confused him. If you ever have a family member that develops Alzheimer's, please keep whatever relationship you can with them. And remember that will be harder to do as time goes on.

Michele visited her mom just before Christmas in 2023. She wasn't doing well, and her blood pressure was very low. "I held Mom's hand and told her it was all right to go if that's what she wanted to do."

She kissed her mom goodbye and left. Two days later, the day after Christmas, Michele and her dad got a call telling them that Annette had just died. "Mom came to me in a dream that night. She looked like she'd looked years ago. She told me not to worry, that she was doing all right. That made me happy. I'm glad she's at peace."

LATE-STAGE ALZHEIMER'S (SEVERE)

In this stage, people with Alzheimer's can no longer respond to their environment, carry on a conversation, and sometimes cannot control their movements. Significant personality changes take place, and people in this stage usually need twenty-four-hour care. They lose memory of recent experiences and forget their surroundings. They lose the ability to walk, sit, and even to swallow. Even though people with late-stage Alzheimer's can no longer interact with others, they may benefit by listening to relaxing music or receiving comfortable touches such as holding hands. This stage is when some families consider placing the person with Alzheimer's in hospice care, which can benefit families as well as patients.

The Stigma of Alzheimer's Disease

Stigma is the negative perception that people with particular conditions, such as mental health issues, addiction, or other conditions may experience. It can happen to people with Alzheimer's as well as to their caregivers. Misconceptions and lack of public awareness about the condition may cause people to delay seeking medical care when symptoms first occur. A delay in an early Alzheimer's diagnosis can affect a person's later quality of life. This includes how a person plans or prepares for their future, how they may benefit from available treatments, or how they can develop a support system among family and friends.

The Alzheimer's Association Early-Stage Advisory Group, made up of people in the early stage of Alzheimer's, offers five tips for people living with Alzheimer's on raising awareness of the disease to combat stigma:

1. **Be open and direct.** Engage others in discussions about Alzheimer's disease.
2. **Communicate the facts.** Sharing accurate information is key to dispelling misconceptions about the disease.

3. **Seek support and stay connected.** It is important to stay engaged in meaningful relationships and activities.
4. **Don't be discouraged.** Denial of the disease by others is not a reflection of you. If people think that Alzheimer's disease is normal aging, see it as an education opportunity.
5. **Be part of the solution.** As an individual living with the disease, yours is the most powerful voice to help raise awareness, end stigma, and advocate for more Alzheimer's support and research.

One does not actually need to be a person living with Alzheimer's or know someone living with Alzheimer's to engage in these tips to raise awareness. Anybody can help dispel stigma against Alzheimer's disease.

Take Care of Your Brain

Scientists don't yet know exactly what causes Alzheimer's disease, which makes it impossible to prevent. But the Alzheimer's Association suggests ways to help people reduce the risk of cognitive decline regardless of the cause. These activities will help both the brain and the body:

- **Break a sweat.** Engage in regular cardiovascular exercise. This increases blood flow to the heart as well as the brain.
- **Hit the books.** Education helps improve brain function. Take a class at school or online. Brush up on an old skill or learn a new language.
- **Stump yourself.** Challenges such as jigsaw puzzles, card games, or chess are good for the mind. Participating in challenging cognitive activities can reduce the risk of developing dementia for people over the age of seventy by up to 11 percent.

Early-Stage Advisory Group

The Alzheimer's Association is looking for people to join their early-stage advisory group. If you know of someone with early-stage Alzheimer's, consider telling them about this group. It provides a unique opportunity for the person to turn their experience into inspiration for others living with the disease. Their voices and actions are powerful tools that can help raise awareness of Alzheimer's to empower others. The group focuses on four activities:

1. Increasing public concern and awareness in media outlets, such as the *New York Times* and NBC Nightly News
2. Enhancing care and support of people with early-stage Alzheimer's with online tools and articles
3. Advancing public policy by testifying to the US Social Security Administration and working with the National Alzheimer's Project Act Advisory Council
4. Accelerating research by working with the National Institutes of Health and the Food and Drug Administration (FDA)

- **Catch some z's.** Getting enough sleep each night helps prevent problems with memory and thinking.
- **Buddy up.** Support brain health by staying socially active and engaging in interests with others. Visit friends, volunteer at a local animal shelter, join a community choir, or start a book club.
- **Fuel up well.** Stick to a diet that's low in fat and has plenty of fruits and vegetables.

Dr. C. Kathleen Dorey, professor at Virginia Tech Carilion School of Medicine, led a 2023 study emphasizing the value of a balanced diet high in fruits and vegetables. The study looked at the brains of more than thirty individuals, most of whom had Alzheimer's. The brains of those with Alzheimer's had half the level of certain vital nutrients compared to the brains of people without Alzheimer's. Dorey said, "This study, for the first time, demonstrates deficits in important dietary antioxidants in Alzheimer's brains."

Antioxidants are substances that work to prevent oxidation in the body, which can damage living cells. Only very small amounts of the following nutrients are needed for maximum brain function:

- **Lycopene.** This nutrient improves heart health and lowers the risk of developing certain types of cancer. It gives some fruits and vegetables their red color. Tomatoes, watermelons, pink grapefruit, and guavas are all high in lycopene.

In 2023 the Harvard TH Chan School of Public Health released a study that looked at the diets of more than 240,000 people. Those who adhered to a diet low in meat and saturated fats, and high in plant-based foods, had a lower risk of developing Alzheimer's disease and other forms of dementia.

- **Retinol, a form of vitamin A.** This helps the immune system work and promotes good eyesight. The body converts nutrients from certain fruits and vegetables into retinol. The body can process yellow, red, and leafy green vegetables, such as spinach, carrots, red peppers, sweet potatoes, and yellow fruits, such as mangoes and apricots, into retinol.
- **Lutein.** This helps protect the eye from the sun and improves vision. Lutein is in kale, egg yolks, spinach, corn, orange peppers, kiwis, squash, and grapes.
- **Zeaxanthin.** This also helps protects the eyes. It can be found in eggs, oranges, grapes, corn, mangoes, and orange peppers.
- **Vitamin E.** This antioxidant helps improve immune function and prevents blood clots in the heart. Nuts, seeds, and fruits and vegetables, including spinach, pumpkin, red bell peppers, asparagus, mangoes, and avocados all contain vitamin E.

Next Steps

There are many ways to take care of your brain's health. Even so, it's impossible to entirely prevent Alzheimer's disease. Knowing what is likely to happen in the middle and late stages of Alzheimer's disease lets people prepare for what happens next. That can include taking classes in communication and caregiving for those with Alzheimer's. Many Alzheimer's patients are diagnosed in the early stages of their illness. Recent improvements in diagnostic testing can help ensure that patients get the best care they need at the time they need it.

Alzheimer's and Brain Awareness Month

Support the Alzheimer's Association's Alzheimer's and Brain Awareness Month each June. The association encourages people to look for ways to raise money to support Alzheimer's research. The organization says, "The day with the most light is the day we fight. On June 21—the summer solstice—people from across the world will fight the darkness of Alzheimer's through a fundraising activity of their choice."

Wear a purple "The Longest Day" T-shirt while doing an activity to support the cause. The organization provides information on how to turn the activity into a fundraiser with mobile apps, posters and flyers, email templates, and more.

Your parents or guardians can help by asking if their employers will match contributions they make to charitable causes. You can tell teachers you'd like to give a talk about Alzheimer's and to collect donations. Funds go toward research, prevention, and treating Alzheimer's disease, and can further the rights and meet the needs of people with the condition.

People gathered in West Palm Beach, Florida, in 2019 to participate in a Walk to End Alzheimer's event to raise money and awareness for Alzheimer's disease.

CHAPTER 4

Diagnosis and Treatment

If I get dementia, remember that I am still the person you know and love.
—Rachael Wonderlin, dementia consultant

No one wants to hear a doctor say their loved one has Alzheimer's disease. Yet there are benefits to receiving a diagnosis of Alzheimer's as early as possible. Medications started during the early stage are likely to be more effective than if they are started later. The patient also has time to make lifestyle changes, such as treating high blood pressure, which will benefit their general health and possibly delay the progression of Alzheimer's symptoms. An early diagnosis allows the patient to live a mostly normal life at home for longer. It allows families and friends time to plan for the future while the patient can meaningfully participate.

Diagnosing Alzheimer's Disease

For many years, the only certain way to tell if people had Alzheimer's disease was to see the plaques and tangles in their brains at autopsy after their death. Now doctors usually follow a step-by-step process if a patient is exhibiting signs of Alzheimer's disease.

First, patients and their loved ones generally start with their primary care physician (PCP), who asks about the patient's behavior. The PCP checks the patient's medications to see if they might be contributing to the patient's symptoms. The PCP asks if there's a history of dementia in the family and performs a general physical examination. Lab tests can often identify if there is a reversible cause for the dementia.

If the PCP suspects the patient has Alzheimer's or another form of dementia, they will recommend visiting a neurologist, a physician who specializes in diagnosing and treating disorders of the brain and nervous system. The neurologist evaluates the patient for conditions in the brain that may cause dementia, including strokes, tumors, or excessive fluid. The neurologist also performs cognitive tests to evaluate memory and function.

AD8 DEMENTIA SCREENING INTERVIEW

One widely used test is the AD8 Dementia Screening Interview. In this test, the patient, friend, or a family member answers eight questions with yes or no. One point is given for each yes. A score of zero to one means normal cognition. A score of two or above means cognitive impairment is likely present. The doctor asks the patient or family member if they've experienced or witnessed any of the following behaviors over the last year:

1. Problems with judgment (e.g., problems making decisions, bad financial decisions, problems with thinking)?
2. Less interest in hobbies/activities?

3. Repeats the same things over and over (questions, stories, or statements)?
4. Trouble learning how to use a tool, appliance, or gadget (e.g., computer, microwave, remote control)?
5. Forgets correct month or year?
6. Trouble handling complicated financial affairs (e.g., balancing checkbook, income taxes, paying bills)?
7. Trouble remembering appointments?
8. Daily problems with thinking and/or memory?

MINI-COG TEST

Another widely used test to screen for dementia is the Mini-Cog (cognition), which can be administered and graded in just five minutes. The Mini-Cog test is shown on the next two pages.

The Mini-Cog has two parts: a simple memory test and a request to draw a clock with a specific time on it. The doctor will then do the following:

1. Asks the patient to remember three words. For example, they might ask the patient to remember the words *banana*, *sunrise*, and *chair*, chosen from Version 1 on the first page.
2. Asks the patient to draw a clock and to set the hands at a given time. For example, they might say, "Set the hands at ten minutes past three."
3. Lastly, asks the patient what the three words were.

The patient gets one point for each word remembered, one point for drawing the clock, and one point for drawing the time correctly. The maximum score is five. Receiving a score of one or two indicates a higher likelihood of cognitive impairment and possible dementia. A score of three or more suggests a lower likelihood of dementia but may still point toward some cognitive impairment.

Mini-Cog™

Instructions for Administration & Scoring

ID: ____________ Date: ____________________

Step 1: Three Word Registration

Look directly at person and say, "Please listen carefully. I am going to say three words that I want you to repeat back to me now and try to remember. The words are [select a list of words from the versions below]. Please say them for me now." If the person is unable to repeat the words after three attempts, move on to Step 2 (clock drawing).

The following and other word lists have been used in one or more clinical studies.[1-3] For repeated administrations, use of an alternative word list is recommended.

Version 1	Version 2	Version 3	Version 4	Version 5	Version 6
Banana	Leader	Village	River	Captain	Daughter
Sunrise	Season	Kitchen	Nation	Garden	Heaven
Chair	Table	Baby	Finger	Picture	Mountain

Step 2: Clock Drawing

Say: "Next, I want you to draw a clock for me. First, put in all of the numbers where they go." When that is completed, say: "Now, set the hands to 10 past 11."

Use preprinted circle (see next page) for this exercise. Repeat instructions as needed as this is not a memory test. Move to Step 3 if the clock is not complete within three minutes.

Step 3: Three Word Recall

Ask the person to recall the three words you stated in Step 1. Say: "What were the three words I asked you to remember?" Record the word list version number and the person's answers below.

Word List Version: _____ Person's Answers: ________________ ________________ ________________

Scoring

Word Recall: _____ (0-3 points)	1 point for each word spontaneously recalled without cueing.
Clock Draw: _____ (0 or 2 points)	Normal clock = 2 points. A normal clock has all numbers placed in the correct sequence and approximately correct position (e.g., 12, 3, 6 and 9 are in anchor positions) with no missing or duplicate numbers. Hands are pointing to the 11 and 2 (11:10). Hand length is not scored. Inability or refusal to draw a clock (abnormal) = 0 points.
Total Score: _____ (0-5 points)	Total score = Word Recall score + Clock Draw score. A cut point of <3 on the Mini-Cog™ has been validated for dementia screening, but many individuals with clinically meaningful cognitive impairment will score higher. When greater sensitivity is desired, a cut point of <4 is recommended as it may indicate a need for further evaluation of cognitive status.

Clock Drawing

ID: ____________ Date: ____________________

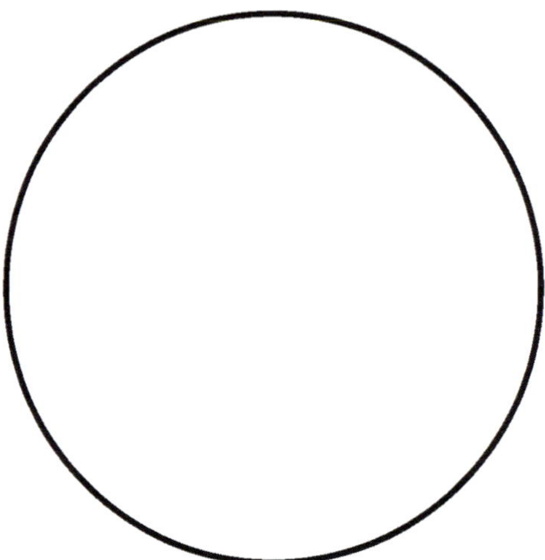

References

1. Borson S, Scanlan JM, Chen PJ et al. The Mini-Cog as a screen for dementia: Validation in a population-based sample. J Am Geriatr Soc 2003;51:1451–1454.
2. Borson S, Scanlan JM, Watanabe J et al. Improving identification of cognitive impairment in primary care. Int J Geriatr Psychiatry 2006;21: 349–355.
3. Lessig M, Scanlan J et al. Time that tells: Critical clock-drawing errors for dementia screening. Int Psychogeriatr. 2008 June; 20(3): 459–470.
4. Tsoi K, Chan J et al. Cognitive tests to detect dementia: A systematic review and meta-analysis. JAMA Intern Med. 2015; E1-E9.
5. McCarten J, Anderson P et al. Screening for cognitive impairment in an elderly veteran population: Acceptability and results using different versions of the Mini-Cog. J Am Geriatr Soc 2011; 59: 309-213.
6. McCarten J, Anderson P et al. Finding dementia in primary care: The results of a clinical demonstration project. J Am Geriatr Soc 2012; 60: 210-217.
7. Scanlan J & Borson S. The Mini-Cog: Receiver operating characteristics with the expert and naive raters. Int J Geriatr Psychiatry 2001; 16: 216-222.

CT, MRI, AND PET SCANS

If the neurologist suspects that the patient may have Alzheimer's disease, the next step is to order one or more brain imaging tests. These can include computerized tomography (CT) scans and magnetic resonance imaging (MRI) scans. The scans can rule out other causes of dementia, such as brain hemorrhages, tumors, or strokes. These scans also show whether parts of the brain have atrophied or shrunk.

A positron emission tomography (PET) scan can show areas of the brain that have been damaged because of poor glucose metabolism. The brain requires continuous glucose and oxygen to function. PETs may strongly suggest, but cannot prove, that a patient has Alzheimer's.

Other PET scans can detect the presence of amyloid or tau tangles using a radioactive substance called a tracer. Doctors do this by injecting tracers into a vein in the patient's arm. The tracers travel through the bloodstream, into the brain, and attach to their target, either amyloid or tau. Then the doctor scans the brain to see where the tracers are. Different agents are used to detect amyloid and tau. These forms of PET scans allow physicians to make a diagnosis of possible Alzheimer's disease.

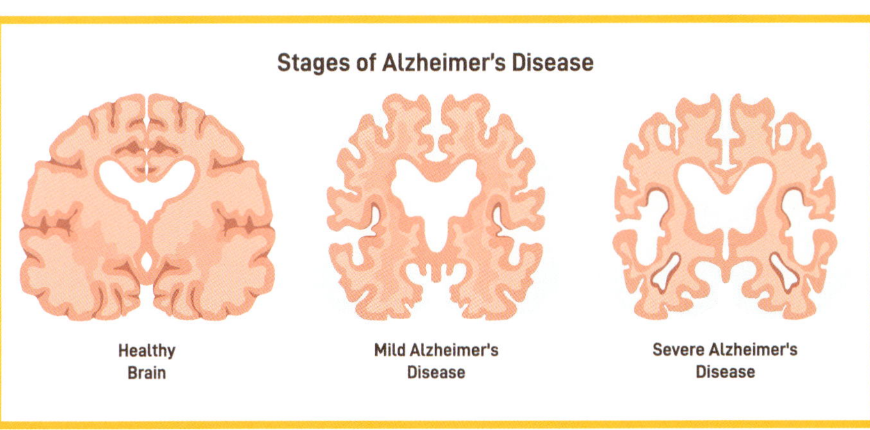

As Alzheimer's progresses, brain cells die, and the brain shrinks. CT, MRI, and PET scans can show this shrinkage.

Amyloid Plaques and Tau Tangles

Plaques form when sticky pieces of the protein beta-amyloid clump together in the brain between nerve cells, hampering communication between the cells. Tangles form when the protein tau collects inside of nerve cells, blocking nutrients needed to nourish the cells.

One study found tau in the brains of everyone over the age of fifty-five, including those without dementia. A different study by researchers at Maastricht University in the Netherlands sampled nearly twenty thousand participants and estimated that over one-third of seemingly unimpaired people over the age of seventy have amyloid in their brains.

The presence of amyloid or tau does not necessarily point to Alzheimer's disease. Even so, the greater the amount present on a PET scan, the greater the likelihood that the individual has Alzheimer's.

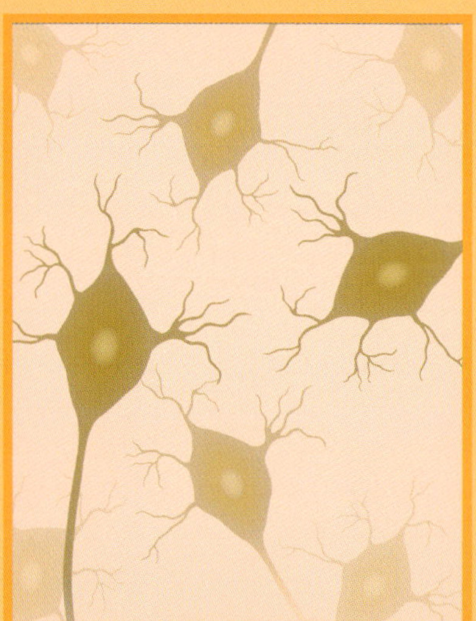

Illustrations of nerve cells in a healthy brain (*left*) and in a brain with Alzheimer's (*right*) that shows amyloid plaques

CSF AND BLOOD TESTS

Another way to diagnose Alzheimer's disease is by testing cerebrospinal fluid (CSF). CSF is the clear fluid that surrounds and protects the brain and spinal cord. It also carries nutrients throughout the brain. Doctors perform a lumbar puncture, or spinal tap, to take a sample of a patient's CSF. The patient lies on their side with their legs drawn up. The doctor numbs an area on the back before inserting a needle into the space between two vertebrae and withdrawing a sample of CSF. A laboratory tests the CSF to see how much amyloid and tau are present.

In recent years, companies have developed several blood tests to identify Alzheimer's. As blood circulates through the body, it picks up traces of damaged amyloid and tau from the brain. These blood tests identify those traces, which helps doctors diagnose Alzheimer's. The National Institutes of Health funded a study that sampled the blood of fifty-three people with Alzheimer's disease and mild cognitive impairment and found traces of amyloid in fifty-two of them. This is more accurate than testing CSF. These blood tests may replace CSF testing entirely as they are easier for doctors to perform, although none have been approved yet by the FDA.

Several similar tests are on the horizon. Compared to CT, MRI, and PET scans, blood tests are faster, less expensive, and don't expose patients to unnecessary radiation. At the July 2023 Alzheimer's Association International Conference, researchers from the University of Gothenburg in Sweden reported—for the first time—that a simple finger prick blood test, similar to what people with diabetes do daily, shows promise in detecting Alzheimer's by identifying amyloid in the blood.

Another finger-prick blood test in development will show both amyloid and tau in patients' blood. PCPs would perform this test in their office. A study conducted by Lund University in Sweden showed that PCPs had correctly identified Alzheimer's patients in about 55 percent of cases in the study by conventional methods, but

The BrainSee Test

In January 2024, the FDA approved a new test called BrainSee that can be given to people with memory loss. Patients undergo an MRI scan and take a cognitive test. BrainSee, an artificial intelligence (AI)–based medical software, then analyzes the results of the scan and the test and predicts the likelihood of that patient's condition progressing to Alzheimer's within five years. It assigns a score, ranging from zero to one hundred. The higher the score, the greater the risk that a person will develop Alzheimer's. After a five-year study with 107 patients, BrainSee was 91 percent accurate in predicting Alzheimer's.

the blood test was accurate more than 80 percent of the time. Dr. Sebastian Palmqvist, one of the scientists at Lund University involved in researching the blood tests, said, "Blood tests for Alzheimer's disease have great potential for improving diagnostic accuracy and proper treatment of people with Alzheimer's. These tests may become even more important in the near future, as new drugs that slow down the disease in its early stages become more widely available."

Dr. Gil Rabinovici, who directs the Alzheimer's Disease Research Center at the University of California, San Francisco, remarked that these new blood tests are a big advance in Alzheimer's research. "It's something that five years ago I would have thought was science fiction," he said. In 2019 Rabinovici published a study sampling more than eleven thousand patients who had "early memory or thinking changes with an uncertain cause." In the study, PET imaging of the brain discovered that 25 percent of people who were believed to have Alzheimer's did not have it. And 10 percent who were not believed to have Alzheimer's *did* have it. Accurate diagnoses are critical for providing correct treatments. With the success blood tests have had, physicians may soon adopt them as a regular part of their diagnostic routine.

BOBBIE'S STORY: My Husband Has Alzheimer's

Until Bobbie Brubaker's husband, David, was diagnosed with Alzheimer's disease, it seemed that his mind had been just fine. Then she began to see changes.

> **At first it was little things that I noticed and easily dismissed as normal aging. Sadly, that was not the case. David kept forgetting things and making mistakes. For example, he returned a bill he intended to pay without including the check. He'd never done anything like that before.**
>
> **David told his primary care physician about his forgetfulness and the doctor gave him the Mini-Cog test to test his memory. David failed the test, and the doctor told us David likely had Alzheimer's disease. We went to see an Alzheimer's specialist who said based on the Mini-Cog, David had mild cognitive impairment. He ordered an MRI. The result was a real red flag. It showed us what had already taken place and what would be happening in the future.**

Bobbie is a nurse, and she knew that MRIs could show if areas of the brain have shrunken. But while evidence of brain shrinkage tells a doctor that the patient might have Alzheimer's, it cannot provide an absolute diagnosis.

> **David developed prostate cancer as well, so we left our home in Sutter Creek [California] and moved to San Francisco, where he could get treatment for both his cancer and his Alzheimer's. We moved into an assisted-living facility there. The treatment for David's cancer was successful. For a couple of years, we lived at that facility where we had a decent apartment. We could stick to a**

routine. I would make dinner, and we had breakfast and lunch downstairs in the dining hall. David used the facility gym, and we went out into the city and walked a lot because there's so much to do in San Francisco.

Then the COVID-19 pandemic struck the world in 2020.

We lived through some difficult times. The worst was that David couldn't understand why we couldn't go out during the pandemic. This was the breaking point, when he wouldn't listen to me but instead got angry and argued with me. I had to place him in a local memory care facility in 2021. He knows he has a poor memory, but he can't understand why he's living in a new place. I visited daily at first to help get him acclimated and it exhausted me!

David Brubaker loves music. Every Sunday at Golden Gate Park in San Francisco, a band plays. Bobbie takes him there to listen as his disease progresses. His love for music seems to be one of the few things he remembers.

David's place is okay. Things that come up are usually surprising but should have been foreseen. For example, he escaped from the facility two times. Once he followed someone who was leaving the building, and another time he got out through a back door, which is now barricaded. I found pills in his pocket. When I asked why he wasn't

"With dementia, the best thing to do is to give a simple explanation, without talking down to the person."

—Bobbie Brubaker

taking his medication, David said they gave him too many pills and he didn't need them. He doesn't like the facility because he's locked in, and he feels some of the staff treat him like an idiot. I wish there was more oversight, but this was the best place of the six I looked at. I try to keep the staff on their toes without making waves. That can be tricky. But no place is perfect.

With dementia, the best thing to do is to give a simple explanation, without talking down to the person. David always has some level of suspicion about what's going on around him. I try to stick to the truth without going into major details. That usually works. But sometimes, telling white lies, like you're on the waiting list for a room on another floor, keeps him calm. The gist of it for me is that his needs are paramount. As long as I have friends and exercise outlets, I can deal with almost anything.

While David's primary care doctor diagnosed Alzheimer's based on the Mini-Cog test, it's *not* a test for Alzheimer's disease. According to Soo Borson, MD, developer of the Mini-Cog test, "The Mini-Cog is a short test for cognitive impairment and dementia. You can think of it as something like a searchlight—it doesn't tell you exactly what's happening, but it can indicate a need for a more thorough evaluation."

Poetry about Alzheimer's

Eugenia Zukerman is an internationally known flutist, journalist, and author. She wrote the poem "Marbles" two years after being diagnosed with Alzheimer's.

"Marbles"

Maybe mine are lost
or maybe they're rolling around
in my head looking for a place to land
Or maybe not
my daughters tell me to get tested
tested for what I ask
even though I know for what
but it's for what I don't want to know
So I let the marbles roll around
in a swirl of distracting colors
because I don't want to listen to them
the daughters
because if I hear them
I will
be
very afraid
and this mother cannot be that mother
not ever
never

Treatments for Alzheimer's Disease

Even though Alzheimer's cannot be *cured*, extensive research has led to the development of a medication that *delays* the progression of cognitive and memory decline. In 2023 the FDA approved lecanemab (brand name Leqembi), a type of medication that targets amyloid. It is given intravenously, or into the vein such as through an IV or needle, every two weeks. In a study of nearly eighteen hundred patients, half received Leqembi while the other half received a placebo (a harmless medicine that would not affect Alzheimer's but is believed by the patient to be Leqembi), so that the study would have a control group. All the patients had early Alzheimer's disease with mild dementia. Tracked over eighteen months, patients who received Leqembi experienced a 27 percent decrease in the decline of their cognitive skills.

Joanne Pike, president of the Alzheimer's Association, said in a press release about Leqembi, "This treatment, while not a cure, can give people in the early stages of Alzheimer's more time to maintain their independence and do the things they love. This gives people more months of recognizing their spouse, children, and grandchildren. This also means more time for a person to drive safely, accurately and promptly take care of family finances, and participate fully in hobbies and interests."

But while Leqembi slows down cognitive decline by about five months, many private insurers are reluctant to cover its yearly cost of $26,000, according to a Public Broadcasting Service health column. Some insurance companies view the medication as still experimental and believe the risks outweigh the benefits. Some prefer to wait to see the results of further testing. But Medicare, the federal health insurance for people aged sixty-five and older and younger people with qualifying disabilities, plans on covering most of the cost for Alzheimer's patients.

Researchers have also looked into medications that help clear tau. But, according to a study published in the *Journal of the American Geriatrics Society*, evidence shows that removal of tau had little effect on the patient's cognitive ability. This makes anti-amyloid medications the only ones shown to improve patient functioning when given early in the course of the disease.

Some patients also benefit by taking medications that help behavior, rather than cognition. For example, some patients don't sleep well, so doctors may prescribe medications for insomnia. Other medications given for behavioral symptoms include those that reduce agitation and depression, as well as antipsychotic medications that help decrease delusions and hallucinations. The Alzheimer's Association advises that "due to the serious side effects of [medications such as antipsychotics], it is essential that their use is closely monitored. It is also recommended that the person stay on the medications only for as long as necessary."

CARLIE'S STORY: My Grandpa Steve Had Alzheimer's Disease

Carlie Sokol is in her early twenties, but she was a teen when she learned that her grandpa had Alzheimer's disease.

When my mom told me that my grandpa Steve had Alzheimer's disease, I didn't believe it at first. I knew Grandpa was a quiet guy, but I'd gotten used to this personality change over the years. Grandpa was a very quirky man. He had an aquarium in his basement, and he gave me chocolate chips that he called medicine.

As he started developing Alzheimer's disease, he slowly became less talkative. I remember when he showed signs of his past self, like when he sang along to a song perfectly, or when he played ping-pong without missing a beat. One of the hardest parts of Grandpa's Alzheimer's for me was when he went missing one day. My mom and I drove around the streets of San Francisco hoping to find my lost and confused grandpa. The police found him, and he was okay. Even though he was all right, it was a scary moment, and it was hard to see my mom go through it.

Once his Alzheimer's became too much for my nana Linda to handle at home, the family moved Grandpa into a memory care center. I remember visiting him for his birthday with the whole family, and he seemed like a completely different person from the one I'd known for much of my life. Grandpa deteriorated very quickly, and he forgot how to do a lot of basic activities. The best thing I could do was be there to support my mom and Nana Linda, because I knew it was the hardest on them.

Steve Lyon (*left*) in a memory care facility in the San Francisco area with his wife, Linda Kosut Lyon (*right*)

Carlie's grandfather Steve has been gone for several years now. She wants young people to know that Alzheimer's is very common. "If someone you love is affected, you are not alone. Feeling forgotten by your loved one is very hard, so it's important to remember how they used to be and to cherish your favorite memories of them," she said.

> **"As he started developing Alzheimer's disease, he slowly became less talkative. I remember when he showed signs of his past self, like when he sang along to a song perfectly, or when he played ping-pong without missing a beat."**
>
> —*Carlie Sokol*

In Denial?

Accepting a diagnosis of Alzheimer's disease is likely to be one of the toughest challenges that affected people and their families will ever face. It may take time and patience for affected people to work through their grief and shock at learning they have an incurable condition. The Alzheimer's Association offers some suggestions for coping:

- Provide time for the individual to feel sad about how [their] identity is changing as a result of the diagnosis.
- Emphasize the roles and responsibilities that are still significant to the individual's identity. I.e., grandfather, mother, daughter, etc.
- Encourage the person to speak with a trusted friend, minister, or even a professional counselor, to talk through difficult emotions.

Why is it so important to process and accept the diagnosis? So far, medications that the FDA has approved for people with Alzheimer's disease work best when started at the earliest possible time—preferably in the early stage. The sooner a patient accepts a diagnosis, the sooner they can participate in their own treatment.

The Ongoing Search for New Treatments

New ways to diagnose and treat Alzheimer's are likely to revolutionize treatment of the condition in coming years. Research has progressed to where scientists can think about addressing the underlying causes of Alzheimer's. According to Alzheimer's Los Angeles, "In ongoing clinical trials, scientists are developing and testing several possible interventions, including immunization therapy, drug therapies, cognitive training, physical activity, and treatments for cardiovascular disease and diabetes." All of these will help, but meanwhile, learning how to best care for Alzheimer's patients is essential.

CHAPTER 5

Caring for Alzheimer's Patients

If I get dementia and I live in a dementia care community, please visit me often.
—Rachael Wonderlin, dementia consultant

People that currently have a loved one with Alzheimer's disease might feel overwhelmed. They might not know anything about helping an Alzheimer's patient. They may ask themselves: What if we mess up? Where will they go? Who will take care of them? And how will the family be able to pay for the needed care? How can they figure out what to do next? So many questions!

Once the Alzheimer's specialist doctor has talked to a patient's family, the next step for the family is to learn everything they can about Alzheimer's disease. This can help the family make the right decisions at the right time. Local chapters of the Alzheimer's Association and many other groups can help. Family members and loved ones can take in-person or online classes. They can join local support groups and talk to other people who are in a similar situation. The National Council on Aging can help families find financial resources. With these resources, people can find many of the answers they want and get the help they need.

It can be very difficult for people to discover that someone they care for has Alzheimer's disease. They may be shocked or saddened by the diagnosis. Many people go through the stages of grief when they first find out. People may not experience these emotions in this order, or they may not experience each stage. But many go through the following stages of grief:

- **Denial.** Hoping the person is not really ill or expecting them to get better
- **Anger.** Frustration with the person and the demands of caregiving if you become the primary or secondary caregiver
- **Guilt.** Thinking you didn't do something that might have helped prevent their dementia
- **Sadness.** Feeling overwhelmed or upset about what's happening
- **Acceptance.** Learning to live in the moment and finding meaning by helping the person with Alzheimer's

It is hard to know who is likely to be diagnosed with Alzheimer's disease or when. But people can do things to help when someone they love receives a diagnosis, whether they're a primary or secondary caregiver, or a concerned loved one. An estimated 6.9 million people ages sixty-five and over live with Alzheimer's disease, with many millions more family members and loved ones supporting them, so they're not alone.

Where to Go?

Once a patient has been diagnosed with Alzheimer's disease, the next question is where they should go. Or do they even *need* to go anywhere? The answer depends on how much help they require. Patients with mild, or early-stage, Alzheimer's can often remain in their own homes, and family members can help them. Family members might also consider hiring somebody to provide homemaker (companion) services for the patient. This helps a person with Alzheimer's complete household tasks that they can't complete alone, such as cooking and cleaning.

People with moderate, or middle-stage, Alzheimer's might stay at home or live with their caregiver, who is often a close family member. But they may go to day care centers for Alzheimer's patients for several hours a day, a few days a week. There, patients receive care, while the primary or secondary caregiver has time to recuperate. Caregiving can be intensive, and can be hard on the caregiver's mental and physical state. Having help from multiple resources helps support them too. Meanwhile, the patient may enjoy the new surroundings and company that comes with these day care centers. If that doesn't work, some families hire in-home health-care workers such as home health aides to help either full-time or for a few hours a day.

Patients in the late stage of Alzheimer's may benefit from living in an adult family home, which is a private home for Alzheimer's patients with staff to assist them as needed around the clock. Other people may decide to place their family member with Alzheimer's in a memory care facility, designed to provide a safe and structured environment for people with Alzheimer's. A memory care facility is a place where people with Alzheimer's disease can live safely. The facility may have just a few rooms or dozens of rooms. Many times, these rooms look like apartments. Regardless of the size, a memory care facility provides

Activities for Alzheimer's Patients

Abaigeal (Abby) Johnson has worked with Alzheimer's patients for several years. She's a former activity director and current care coordinator at a memory care facility near Sacramento, California. Some of the activities she's organized that residents enjoy most are art, music, and learning about AI technology. "Every day I make a difference in people's lives," Abby says. "For example, I taught an eighty-seven-year-old to paint with watercolors for the first time. The residents especially enjoy listening to live music. We have a musician who visits and sings to groups while he plays his guitar. We encourage residents to sing along with the music. Another fun project was introducing AI technology to a group of seniors and watching their faces light up as the AI wrote stories in seconds based on a few prompts from their own lives."

Abby Johnson, Terrace Club care coordinator

Abby believes that activities are very important for residents affected by all kinds of dementias, especially Alzheimer's. "Activity programs should be personalized, planned to engage a group or an individual, and set people up for success," she says. "Activities can add a sense of purpose and fulfillment to people's lives. Such programs should offer activities in multiple areas, including spiritual, reflection, learning, physical, nature, and animals. Activities should give participants a sense of pride and accomplishment." Well-planned programs improve the quality of life for residents and can also improve sleep. "My favorite question from a resident is, 'What are we going to do today?' Activity programs give seniors a purposeful life and a reason to keep on going."

twenty-four-hour care by specially trained staff. Exit doors are locked, and residents cannot leave the facility without a family or staff member. This helps prevent cases of wandering. Most memory care facilities provide physical and social activities that benefit Alzheimer's patients. Some facilities also provide independent living and assisted living for residents who need little or no supervision.

Care in Stages

EARLY-STAGE ALZHEIMER'S

Many people who are in the early, or mild, stage of Alzheimer's can still function mostly independently, so it can be a challenge to figure out how much help they need. They may be able to complete most daily activities with minimal supervision. Some people with early-stage Alzheimer's may still be able to drive and work. They can also participate in family activities. The Alzheimer's Association says that caregivers may need to help someone in early-stage Alzheimer's keep appointments, recall names and places, plan and organize their time, and keep track of medications. It's especially important to be certain the person can still manage their household finances.

Knowing what the future may hold allows people with early Alzheimer's and their loved ones time to plan for that future. People can begin to figure out where and how they'll live as the condition progresses. Families can think about how much care may cost and what private insurance, Medicare, and Social Security will cover. Does your loved one have a will? Who has power of attorney—the legal right to make decisions for patients once they are no longer capable of doing so on their own? You and your family can also learn about available medications and treatments.

MIDDLE-STAGE ALZHEIMER'S

Patients will need more care during this period. People with middle-stage Alzheimer's are likely to mix up words. They may refuse to bathe.

They may repeat themselves over and over again. Eating and dressing can be difficult. Sleep problems become common. Wandering inside a store, through the house, or out the front door without a purpose is also common. They may grow frustrated, angry, depressed, or anxious. There will be good days and not-so-good days.

One way to help the patient is to offer limited choices. This reduces confusion. Don't ask, "What do you want to wear today?" Instead, lay out clothing for the day on a bed—in the order it should be put on. Don't ask, "What do you want for lunch?" Instead ask, "Do you want a tuna sandwich or a grilled cheese?"

Keep the table setting simple by avoiding dishes with color and patterns. Try offering only one food at a time—for example, vegetables, mashed potatoes, then sliced chicken. Plan activities for the day. You could take a walk, watch a TV show, or garden together. This can help reduce behaviors such as wandering and agitation.

Mealtimes can be difficult for people with Alzheimer's. Here are six tips from the National Institute on Aging for how to make it easier:

People with middle-stage Alzheimer's will have reduced memory and decision-making skills. Because of this, it may no longer be safe for them to drive. The patient might be confused at first or grow frustrated with not being allowed to drive. If that happens, try to explain why it's no longer possible for them to drive and seek their agreement.

As the patient's condition progresses, their immediate safety can be a concern. For example, people with Alzheimer's are likely to wander, may forget how to use common household appliances, and are at risk of falling. People should no longer live alone at this stage. This is the time to consider having the person live with relatives or loved ones. Maybe it's time to consider moving into a memory care facility.

Home Care Safety Tips

Take a look around your house to see what might be potentially harmful. If you and your family have a loved one with Alzheimer's at home, following home care safety tips can help keep the person safe. The Alzheimer's Association provides a Home Safety Checklist to help you keep every room safe. These are just a few of the tips they recommend:

- Store potentially hazardous items, such as medication, alcohol, matches, sharp objects, or small appliances and tools, in a securely locked cabinet.
- Remove tripping hazards, such as throw rugs, extension cords, and excessive clutter.
- Install a latch or deadbolt either above or below eye level on all doors leading outside.
- Install grab bars for the shower, tub, and toilet to provide additional support.
- Remove access to car keys if the individual living with dementia can no longer drive.
- Apply stickers to glass doors at eye level to ensure doors are visible.

Cost of Care

Caregiving can be costly, and the cost will depend on the type of care a person with Alzheimer's receives. Memory care is a common type of care for people with Alzheimer's disease. In 2023 the national median cost for memory care was $5,995 per month. But some memory care communities can cost as much as $10,000 or more a month depending on geographical location, types of amenities, amount of care needed, and size of living space.

The costs can make planning for caregiving tough financially. Many caregivers pay for memory care using their personal savings, the patient's Social Security benefits, or retirement funds from a former job. Some long-term health insurance providers will reimburse the cost of memory care, although many policies don't cover the full cost. Medicare may cover the cost of physical therapy and some prescription medicine. Caregivers can research ways to ease their financial burden by exploring resources such as BenefitsCheckUp, a government service that helps find benefit programs, and Eldercare Locator, which connects a person to caregiving services in their local community.

Cost of care for Alzheimer's patients in 2023

TYPE OF CARE	MONTHLY COST*
Adult day care services	$2,058
Homemaker (companion) services	$5,200
Home health aide	$5,720
Assisted living community	$5,350
Memory care	$5,995

*National median costs

Sources: "Cost of Care Survey," Genworth, December 2023, https://www.genworth.com/aging-and-you/finances/cost-of-care.
Haines Eason, "Everything You Need to Know About the Cost of Memory Care: A State-by-State Guide," A Place for Mom, accessed April 16, 2024, https://www.aplaceformom.com/caregiver-resources/articles/cost-of-memory-care.

LATE-STAGE ALZHEIMER'S

People with late-stage Alzheimer's disease will need help with all activities of daily living because their memory is severely impaired. They may need assistance walking, and in the very late stage, they may be unable to walk even with assistance. Infections such as pneumonia are a constant threat. The patient will have problems with eating and even swallowing. Caregivers responsible for helping people with Alzheimer's to eat must be very careful. For example, patients should be in a comfortable upright position. Offer soft foods that are easy to swallow such as yogurt and pudding. Thicken fluids, such as milk, soup, and juices, with cornstarch or a product available at a drugstore to reduce the chance of choking on liquids. Encourage self-feeding or assist as needed. Patients may need reminders to chew or swallow. It will also be helpful to monitor their weight. A person with late-stage Alzheimer's is likely to lose weight due to eating difficulties.

During the late stage, patients continue to experience the world mainly through their five senses. Caregivers can offer support through touch, sound, sight, taste, and smell. Activities that engage the senses include playing favorite music, reading aloud, looking at old photos together, offering favorite foods, smelling flowers, brushing hair, and gently massaging the hands with lotion. These activities are likely to benefit patients. Even if the Alzheimer's patient no longer recognizes a person, they may still be able to connect with them.

Families may consider putting their loved one on hospice, which can be at home or in a facility. The patient may stop receiving medications and treatment. Patients on hospice will still receive other care, but the focus is now on their quality of life. Hospice care ensures that the patient remains comfortable in the last few weeks or months of their life, often in the comfort of their home with loved ones. Ideally, discussions about what to do at the end of life would have taken place much earlier.

No matter what the stage, caregivers can focus on maintaining the quality of life and the dignity of people with Alzheimer's.

CHARLIE'S STORY: My Grandmother Had Alzheimer's Disease

Charlie Poole's grandmother Helen Pomakoy had Alzheimer's. Charlie remembers how his family used to visit her, especially on holidays.

Before my grandma moved in with us, we would visit her several times every year. She lived in Illinois, about a twelve-hour drive from our house in Virginia. Our grandma loved celebrating and decorating for big holidays, so it was always fun being with her.

I remember starting to notice that every time we visited, Grandma spent less time with the family and more time alone in her room. At first, I thought this was because Grandma was getting older and was simply more tired now. But when we talked to her or woke her up for dinner, she always seemed surprised to see us. She'd forgotten we were there! She would forget to feed her dog, and she left things around her house in strange places. I remember feeling sad, but it didn't occur to me that her behavior was the result of an illness.

When I first learned my grandmother had Alzheimer's, I didn't understand the scope of her condition and how it would unfold over the next few years. It was really hard for me to hear her diagnosis and to realize that she would never get any better. This wasn't something like a normal disease or illness, where after some treatment or medication she would get back to normal. Even good care only delayed the symptoms. I would have been better prepared if I'd actually known how the disease would eventually progress.

When Charlie was twelve and his younger brother, AJ, was ten, their grandmother Helen moved into their house and the brothers helped take care of her.

Both of our parents worked away from home and didn't get home until late afternoon. So, during the daytime when they were gone, it was up to me and AJ to take care of Grandma. Even when our parents came home, they still had a lot to do in the evenings. We were the ones to give Grandma her medicine and to spend time with her. Becoming a caregiver was a gradual process from when my grandmother first moved in, to when Alzheimer's truly became devastating for her.

The hardest part about caregiving was dealing with situations which had no clear answer. When our grandma was suffering from an acute bout of confusion or memory loss, she would often come upstairs screaming for my mother. This happened most often in the middle of the night, and it occurred a few times a week. Grandma would be belligerent, confused, sad, and a moment later, she'd go back to her own normal self and seemed to be aware of everything. Some nights, she would calm down in thirty minutes. Other nights we would be awake from midnight until 7:00 a.m.

We never ignored Grandma because there was a big chance that she could hurt herself or break things in her confusion. These times were so difficult—along with the sleep deprivation—because we didn't understand why she had those outbursts. All we could do was be with her through the episodes. We had to figure out what the issue was, whether it was real or a product of her mind.

We couldn't just take her back to her room, give her medication, or tell her it's all going to be okay. It could take hours to calm her down.

The best part about caregiving was the fact that our grandma was with us. Instead of driving twelve hours to see her, we could just walk into her room and be with her. She loved Christmas, Halloween, the Fourth of July, and Easter, so we could celebrate all her favorite holidays together. We could be sure that Grandma had everything she needed and was completely safe. Caregiving gave me the assurance that my grandma was being taken care of and that she seemed happy most of the time. The fact that we could contribute to her well-being was an important aspect of caregiving.

Sara Poole, Charlie's mom, wrote about this photo: "I'll never forget this day. Mom was really agitated. In frustration, I handed Charlie a photo album, and he kept her occupied for hours going over photos while I cleaned and did laundry."

I've learned that Alzheimer's disease is not at all how it's generally depicted. The common perception of Alzheimer's from people who haven't experienced it is that it's more like a "quirk" which all elderly people experience at some point. But Alzheimer's is so much more than simple forgetfulness. With the memory loss comes confusion, even in familiar spaces. For example, what was once the bedroom turns into a frightening place. People with Alzheimer's become a completely different person. They may not recognize family members and instead see them as strangers with unknown intentions. This gives them so much stress every day that they may lash out or become depressed. You would fear for your life too if you woke up in these circumstances.

I'm not saying this to scare or demoralize anyone caring for an Alzheimer's patient. Having a good understanding of issues and situations which stem from the memory loss will help you to understand the patient's perspective and allow you to provide better care. If more people understood the depth of this illness, it would be a far more "advocated for" issue than it is currently.

Charlie wants teens to know the impact that youth caregiving can have on a person.

Whenever I talk about caregiving, I always mention how lucky I consider myself to be. My family had both the financial stability and the space at home to accommodate my grandma. There are thousands of caregivers in much worse conditions who still manage to take care of their loved ones. I only had to give up minor things to take care of my grandma, while some teens have to leave school and upend their whole lives in order to help their family members. School is already stressful enough. Imagine having all the responsibilities of being a caregiver on top of that. If you know someone who is a caregiver, be sure to show them understanding. Showing that you recognize their struggles and affirming the work they do can make all the difference in their lives.

I hope I didn't sound too gloomy when I'm talking about Alzheimer's. I want other caregivers to know that what they are doing is worthwhile, even despite the difficulties. You have the opportunity to help loved ones through what's probably the hardest time of their lives. At the same time, you gain memories and experiences that will last for the rest of your life. I'll never regret the decision I made to take care of my grandma, and I hope others feel the same.

Sara Poole's Plan for Caregiving

Sara Poole knew just what she wanted when her mom, Helen, came to live with her, her husband, and her sons, Charlie and AJ.

One of the main reasons we had my mom come live with us was so that she could have the things she wanted for the rest of her days. Living with Alzheimer's is traumatic enough for the person going through it. So it's important to let them keep their lifestyle intact as much as you can. My goal was to be as open as I could be to whatever Mom wanted to do or asked for. I just let her be.

If she wanted cookies? Yes. If she wanted to wash her hair in the kitchen sink? Yes. Diet Coke? Yes. A cigarette? Yes. My personal opinion was to let Mom live as closely as possible to the way she was before the disease took over. If it's unhealthy, who cares? They are alone and confused and dying. Boiled chicken and vegetables aren't going to change that. Cake for dinner? Yes, and I am unapologetic.

Youth Caregivers

Connie Siskowski, PhD, is a registered nurse and the president of the American Association of Caregiving Youth. Keisha L. Jackson is a writer and family caregiver consultant. In a 2021 press release, they wrote:

> **In today's modern society, child and teen caregivers are tackling big challenges against daunting odds, and often without support. They are youth whose strength of character needs to be recognized and valued widely in society.**
>
> **Yet it is ironic that many say young people today are self-centered and irresponsible. Those people don't take into consideration children who assume the adult responsibility of caring for chronically ill, injured, elderly, or disabled family members—parents, grandparents, siblings. They are unaware that there are children who rush home from school, or who are unable to go to school because there's no one else to care for their invalid parent or grandparents. . . .**
>
> **Caregiving youth generally fly under the radar of America's social consciousness. They work behind closed doors, bathing, feeding, giving medications, cooking . . . caring for their loved ones and demonstrating their willingness to put others first.**

MAKING A DIFFERENCE

The Poole family maintains a website that focuses on youth caregiving at https://www.kidsarecaregiverstoo.com/. The Poole brothers write about their experience on the site:

> We helped care for our grandmother at home during the last years of Alzheimer's disease; she died in June 2015. As advocates for kids who are caregivers, our mission is to bring a little bit of happiness to the lives of caregiving youth.
>
> Suppose you are a kid caregiving for someone with Alzheimer's or anything else, like a parent with

> a debilitating disease, mental illness, or addiction. In that case, we know this is probably one of the toughest times of your life. You are not alone. During our caregiving days, it was like nobody understood. Our friends, our teachers, nobody knows what it's like to live with someone who needs a lot of help unless you've been there. Nobody understands like caregivers.

The Poole brothers are active in educating others about Alzheimer's and youth caregiving. The brothers spoke at the 2020 Brain Bowl for Alzheimer's and dementia about caring for their grandmother. The event highlights many nonprofit organizations that focus on raising awareness for neurocognitive disorders, such as Alzheimer's, other dementias, and Parkinson's disease. The brothers represented the American Association of Caregiving Youth at the conference.

Charlie Poole (*right*) at seventeen years old and AJ Poole (*left*) at fifteen years old speaking at the 2020 Brain Bowl in Boca Raton, Florida, about their experience caring for their grandmother

Caregiving for Grandma

The Poole brothers write about their experience caring for their grandmother Helen:

> **She loved cookies. She loved her dog. She liked to watch TV. She knew something was wrong.**
>
> **She loved us. She thanked us a lot. She slept a lot. She was confused. She would not leave the house.**
>
> **She forgot how to use the telephone. She forgot how to use the computer. She forgot how to use a spoon or fork. She would eat with her fingers.**
>
> **She forgot how to use the bathroom. She didn't like to bathe. She wouldn't brush her teeth. It was a ton of work to get her to do these things.**
>
> **She became scared of everything. She would hide. The list is endless. It was hard.**
>
> **It could be funny sometimes. There were good days and really bad, horrible days. I think the hardest part is she forgot who we were.**

Self-Care for Caregivers

It's easy to get absorbed in caring for a loved one with Alzheimer's. But it's important not to forget about self-care. According to the Family Caregiver Alliance, "Caregivers must focus on their own needs, take time for their own health, and get support and respite from caregiving regularly to be able to sustain their well-being during this caregiving journey." Having a loved one be diagnosed with Alzheimer's can be emotionally devastating. The steps that come afterward—finding treatment, moving the patient, and looking after them—can take their toll on caregivers. Because of this, many Alzheimer's organizations offer resources for caregivers.

The journey a person embarks on with their loved one will be difficult—but they don't have to do it alone.

CHAPTER 6

Communication with Alzheimer's Patients

If I get dementia, I don't want to be treated like a child.
Talk to me like the adult that I am.
—Rachael Wonderlin, dementia consultant

Communicating with people who have Alzheimer's can be challenging for both patients and caregivers. People with Alzheimer's have trouble remembering things, and the memory loss only worsens over time. Patients can become agitated, anxious, and angry because they may not understand what's happening. Usually, people have problems finding the words they want to use. And if they speak multiple languages, they may forget all but their first language. Their children and grandchildren may not have learned that language, making communication even more difficult.

Alzheimer's affects everyone differently, but communication problems can generally include the following: not finding the correct word and using familiar words over and over, describing objects rather than calling them by name, losing track of thoughts, gesturing more frequently when they can't find the right word, and speaking less often as the disease progresses.

It's important to remember that the patient is not to blame. Alzheimer's is a degenerative disease. Over time, memory and cognitive functions decline, and in the late stage of Alzheimer's, the patient may not be able to communicate. Even so, don't make assumptions about a person's ability to communicate. Remember that patients with Alzheimer's are trying their best. That means successful communication depends on the caregiver. This requires good listening skills, patience, and understanding. To help the patient, caregivers can do their best to be direct, specific, and positive when communicating with them.

Communication by Stages

The Alzheimer's Association offers advice on how to communicate with Alzheimer's patients depending on what stage of the disease they're in.

THE EARLY STAGE

Many people in the early, or mild, stage of Alzheimer's are still able to fully participate in conversations and engage in social activities. Here are some communication tips for patients in this stage of Alzheimer's:

- Include them in conversations, and speak directly to them rather than to their caregivers.
- Take time to listen as they express their thoughts and feelings.
- Give them time to answer. Don't rush or interrupt them.

- Ask if they'd rather communicate by phone, email, or in person.
- A little humor can lighten the mood and make communication more enjoyable.
- Stay in contact, because your support and friendship are very important to the person with Alzheimer's disease.

THE MIDDLE STAGE

Difficulty in communicating will gradually increase during this stage. Communication tips include the following:

- Seek a quiet place with few distractions when talking to the patient.
- Be sure to speak slowly and clearly.
- Say, "Let's try it this way," rather than pointing out their mistakes.
- Maintain eye contact when you speak to them or when they speak to you. It shows you care.
- Give them time to think about what to say. Patience encourages better communication.
- Ask one question at a time that can be answered with a yes or no.
- Limit choices. Don't ask what they want for dinner. Instead, ask if they want chicken or meatloaf.
- Avoid criticizing or correcting them. Try to figure out what they are saying, and repeat it to help clarify what they mean. Avoid arguing with them.
- Give visual cues to show what you want. For example, if you ask for help in folding the laundry, demonstrate how to fold a towel and say, "Let's do it like this."
- Avoid saying, "I already told you about that" or "Don't you remember?" Instead, repeat yourself if necessary.

HAMZA'S STORY: I Visit People with Alzheimer's Disease

Hamza Najjar doesn't have a family member with Alzheimer's disease, but he's been involved with Alzheimer's patients since he was fourteen and visiting them in memory care centers since he was fifteen. Hamza's cousin Sami told him about a group called the Youth Movement against Alzheimer's (YMAA). That group is now part of a larger organization known as Hilarity for Charity. According to Hilarity for Charity, the two groups "joined forces to engage and activate more young people in our movement to change the trajectory of Alzheimer's disease. Together, we are elevating the national conversation around Alzheimer's, brain health, and prevention to drive awareness and inspire change."

Hilarity for Charity is a nonprofit organization that aims to help families impacted by Alzheimer's and support brain health research. In 2023 Hilarity for Charity held a panel on Alzheimer's prevention moderated by its founders Seth Rogen (*left*) and Lauren Miller Rogen with guests such as neuroscientists Lisa Genova (*center*) and Eseosa Ighodaro (*right*).

Hamza said, "I'd only been in high school for a couple of months and was eager to make my mark and to help change the environment around me. I wondered how important this issue was. I did some research and found statistics that showed Alzheimer's disease is a pressing issue. I learned that my generation is going to be hit the hardest by it if something doesn't change. Once I had the image in my head of friends, cousins, and siblings with Alzheimer's, I decided to take action."

Hamza started his own YMAA club at his high school with the help of his cousin, brother, and best friend.

> **I made this a top priority, and we soon had over seventy active members. I worked with a local tennis academy and helped to put on a tennis tournament. We raised $1,300 and donated it to a local Alzheimer's memory care center.**
>
> **A month later, our YMAA club began to volunteer at the memory care center. Mostly, we just talked to the seniors to give them a taste of the "Youth Gen Z energy" that they miss so much. I enjoyed the work and started volunteering more often there. I began to take on additional responsibility, moving from just talking to the people, to taking care of their basic needs and wheeling them around. The senior I remember most was a Muslim woman named Reema. One day I heard someone speaking Arabic and followed the voice. Reema was trying to communicate with the staff, but she didn't speak English and they didn't speak Arabic. And I do. So, I began translating what Reema was saying. Then I told the staff what she needed. For example, a woman—not a man—must take care of her. She needs to wear her hijab and to pray five times a day. Then I sat with Reema and talked to her. She kept asking for her daughter because she**

Hamza Najjar received a President's Volunteer Service Award when he was sixteen for his work with Alzheimer's patients.

wanted to leave. I felt all the sorrow in the world because I couldn't help her. I never saw Reema again, but she is always in my prayers.

Being a teen caregiver has been challenging. The majority of the seniors I care for don't even remember me, and that makes it tough because you don't know if what you do actually makes a difference. Or it feels that way until you start talking to seniors and cracking jokes. The grins on their faces stretch from ear to ear. At that moment, everything you've done—the time, effort, and energy you've dedicated, becomes worth it.

The time Hamza devoted to YMAA activities created challenges for him. While his grades went down only a little bit, he worried that his friendships had suffered.

Monday through Thursday, I had my whole day planned down to the minute, from 6:00 a.m. to 11:00 p.m. My days were so busy that I just didn't have time for my friends or for personal relationships. Saturday and Sunday were filled with studying and meetings, and Friday with family. That can take a toll on you mentally. Your own support system is crumbling while you're being a support system for others.

Hamza said that when you talk to a person with Alzheimer's disease, you need to break it down and make it as simple as possible. But don't make it too simple, or the senior might feel that you're degrading them.

It's much harder to communicate with those who are farther along in their diagnosis. One helpful thing you can do is to ask them about their past. I used to care for one senior who had been a world-class engineer and traveled all around the world working on projects for big oil companies. Even though he never remembered me, I always asked him about his job. He told me the same thing every time, and as he talked about his past projects and travels, he smiled. That smile made it all worthwhile.

"The grins on their faces stretch from ear to ear. At that moment, everything you've done—the time, effort, and energy you've dedicated, becomes worth it."

—Hamza Najjar

THE LATE STAGE

People in the late stage of Alzheimer's usually require around-the-clock care. The person may rely on nonverbal communication such as facial expressions and sounds, rather than words. Here are some tips to help communicate with patients in this stage:

- Approach them from the front so they can see you, and always identify yourself right away. Don't make them guess who you are, and don't assume they remember you.
- Encourage nonverbal communication using touch, sights, sounds, smells, and taste to aid in communication.
- Try to figure out the feelings behind the words and sounds. Emotions can be more important than words.
- Always treat them with respect and dignity. Remember that it's okay if you don't know what to say. Just being there can be the most important thing.

Communication Tips from the Families

Who better to understand how to communicate with people who have Alzheimer's disease than family members who have or had loved ones with the condition? These recommendations from people who have shared their stories in this book can lessen stress and confusion for people with Alzheimer's:

- **Kevan Atteberry.** "Talk about what the future holds soon after diagnosis. Later on, eliminate phrases like, 'Don't forget,' and 'I already told you,' and 'Don't you remember?'"
- **Bobbie Brubaker.** "Limit giving too much new information at a time because processing is slower. It can be frustrating to share information. Everything needs to slow down. With dementia, a simple explanation, without talking down, is important."

- **Margarita Engle.** "Never argue. For example, Mamá often asks me for her mother's phone number. I used to remind her that my abuelita had been dead for many years. Now I just say, 'I'll give you the number later,' and then change to a cheerful subject."
- **Patty Gregory.** "Meet the person in their world because they cannot enter yours."
- **Michele Langhorst.** "Know what stage a person is in so you know how to talk to them. Mild, moderate, advanced—each stage requires different ways to communicate."
- **Hamza Najjar.** "Whatever you need to tell them, break it down and make it as simple as possible. But keep it to a certain level of complicated; that way it's easy to understand, and the senior doesn't feel like you're degrading them while speaking to them. Remember, they're people too."
- **Charlie Poole.** "Patience is the most important thing when you're taking care of someone with Alzheimer's. People with Alzheimer's are often confused, and it can be very difficult to calm them down. The best thing you can do is to just be with them and talk calmly until they relax. It takes patience to be sure they take their medicine, to help them eat, and to help them with whatever they need. Being patient will not only help the person with Alzheimer's but will also help your own mental health."
- **Carlie Sokol.** "Spend time with the person who has Alzheimer's. Do activities that make them feel connected, such as listening to their favorite music or playing games. Anything that feels familiar to your loved one might let their personality shine through."
- **Mark Zanzinger.** "Be prepared to answer the same question over and over. It can be frustrating, but you've got to be patient."

A Doctor Learns about Communicating

Dr. Sandeep Jauhar is a practicing cardiologist in New York. He's also a public speaker and an author of several books such as *Intern: A Doctor's Initiation*, *Heart: A History*, and *Doctored: The Disillusionment of an American Physician*. Jauhar wrote his fourth book, *My Father's Brain*, about his father's descent into Alzheimer's disease and what he himself learned about the ethical challenges of communicating with patients who have Alzheimer's.

> As a physician who's been trained to level with his patients, to tell them the truth, and to not withhold bad news, I tried to apply this truth-telling paradigm to dementia caregiving, but it just didn't work. I would share uncomfortable truths with my father. He would forget that my mother had died. My siblings would say things like, "Oh, Mom's on her way," or "She's on the airplane and she's coming," and I would tell him, "Dad, no, Mom died. She died three years ago, and nothing we say is going to bring her back." And that would cause him incredible anguish, which he would re-experience every few days when he would ask again, and I would level with him again.
>
> Unfortunately, it took a while, but I came to learn that there's a different conception of dignity when it comes to being an Alzheimer's caregiver. Telling someone the truth isn't the only way to uphold dignity. There's also the idea to meet the person you're caring for where they are in their reality and not forcing them to enter your reality. . . . My father's reality was very different. . . . And so, eventually I came to learn that it's okay to tell little white lies.

KAYLIN'S STORY: My Grandmother Has Alzheimer's Disease

Kaylin Jean-Louis's grandmother, Vera Johnson, has Alzheimer's disease.

> **I was ten years old when I started noticing strange signs in my grandmother. Then my mom told me that my grandmother had Alzheimer's dementia. About a year later, my mom and I decided to move in with my grandmother so we could take care of her in a place that was familiar to her. I had to adjust to a new home and to a new role as a youth caregiver. My mom never forced me to help out, but given the impact my grandmother has had in my life, there was no question that I'd help.**

About a year into caring for her grandmother, Kaylin also began taking care of her great-grandmother, Julie Powell, who had Alzheimer's dementia too. Julie passed away after three years.

Kaylin took her role as a caregiver seriously. "My responsibilities as the secondary caregiver to my grandmother include, but are not limited to, taking her to the bathroom, fixing her meals and snacks,

> "Although her conversations are different, I go right along with her and we laugh and enjoy each other with what we have. Dementia can be very difficult but LOVE is CONSISTENT and it's so much greater than dementia."
>
> *—Priscilla Jean-Louis, Vera Johnson's daughter and Kaylin's mother*

Kaylin Jean-Louis (*left*) at sixteen with her grandmother Vera Johnson. When Kaylin isn't studying at college, she goes home to help care for her grandmother. Kaylin's mother, Priscilla Jean-Louis, coined the phrase "Love is greater than dementia," and puts it on T-shirts.

cleaning up after her, washing dishes, helping with medications, and just watching out to be sure she doesn't hurt herself. My mom, Priscilla, is the primary caregiver, which gives her more responsibility. But I try to do whatever I can to lighten her load and make our caregiving journey easier."

Kaylin noted that communication can be difficult, but it's important to give each other grace. "It can be frustrating when communicating with people who have Alzheimer's," she said. "You cannot always

A Global Effort

Kaylin Jean-Louis posted this message on Facebook for World Alzheimer's Day, September 21, 2023:

> **Today, we make a global effort to raise awareness for those living with Alzheimer's dementia and their caregivers. As a youth caregiver, I can tell you that this journey has had its challenges, but it is all worth it. It means so much to me to have cared for my great-grandmother, Julie Powell, and to care for my grandmother, Vera Johnson, who both had/have Alzheimer's dementia. They cared so much for me, so I dedicated my life to caring for them. Through it all, it has pushed me to raise awareness for others who are in a similar situation as myself. So, today I encourage all caregivers to push through this journey because as my mom says, "Love is truly greater than Dementia."**

understand what they're saying, or why they repeat parts of a conversation several times. Patience makes everything easier and helps you make the most out of the situation."

More important is the love you give and receive from each other.

> **My grandmother brings me joy. We can make her laugh, even if she's not sure what's happening. She loves, loves, loves to talk, so I sit and listen, and react to what she says. She always says, "I love you. Thank you so much for taking care of me." That makes up for the pain of the challenging moments. The most rewarding part about being a young caregiver is having the opportunity to help take care of my grandmother for as long as I can. She did the same for me earlier in her life. Before she got Alzheimer's, my grandmother made it her mission to care for others no matter what, and so taking care of her has helped me keep her legacy alive.**

Someone with Alzheimer's may not remember who you are, but you remember who they are, and you give them the love and care they deserve. She's not her disease. She's not her diagnosis. She's my grandmother. The most challenging part about being a teen caregiver is watching Alzheimer's rob me of time and precious moments with her. It's difficult sometimes when she doesn't recognize me, and I can't talk to her like before.

While there were several challenging moments in my caregiving journey, it didn't heavily affect my school and friendships. My mother made sure that I could still be involved in my school even while being a caregiver. My school gave me credit for community service for my caregiving role. And I earned more hours by being involved in several organizations in my community. Overall, being a teen caregiver has changed my life in many ways, but I wouldn't trade my role in my grandmother's life for anything in the world.

Kaylin wants other teens to know more about youth caregiving.

I want to encourage teens to provide unselfish, loving care to their sick or disabled loved ones. That sacrifice will teach them important life lessons and will make a big difference in their loved ones' lives. Teens should know they're not alone. Youth caregivers are becoming more apparent in our world. And if teens need help, they can reach out to friends and family. They can do Google searches and look for extra support and resources from various organizations. They can even contact me at [my website, Kaylin's Caring Konnection] and ask me questions or to get advice.

Sandeep Jauhar, author of *My Father's Brain*, speaking during a session at the 2022 Jaipur Literature Festival in Jaipur, Rajasthan, in India

The Bottom Line

Communicating with Alzheimer's patients can be rewarding and satisfying. It can also be incredibly challenging. Caregivers and people who work with Alzheimer's patients must also make time for themselves to be most effective. Ask other family members and friends for help. Seek out local organizations to find out what services may be available. Join an Alzheimer's support group, because sharing experiences with people who are going through similar situations can help. People who are calm, rested, and self-assured will be better at communicating with everyone around them, including Alzheimer's patients.

JERI'S STORY: My Husband Had Alzheimer's

Jeri Chase Ferris is a retired teacher and a writer.

> **My husband, Tom, a brilliant teacher and an expert in Russian history, was sixty-eight years old, and he had Alzheimer's. Tom had been diagnosed a couple of years earlier when he began to have paranoid ideas. For example, he believed that the Russian mafia was coming to our house to burn it down and kill us; that family members were calling him on the phone and saying unspeakable things; that I'd let a Russian friend in the house and kept it a secret from him; and that I'd deliberately hung his clothes up out of order.**
>
> **All these beliefs were totally wrong, but I didn't understand what was happening until the possibly real Russian mafia threat. Possibly real because Tom was as pale as a ghost when he told me about it. I took Tom to the police station to report the threat. The police were kind. They said they kept track of the Russian mafia in Los Angeles and these things don't happen. They took me aside and told me that I needed to take Tom to his doctor for a checkup.**

As time went on, Jeri developed ways of communication that helped—at least for a while.

> **I found new ways to talk with Tom. We needed to be alone without distractions. I couldn't suggest several things at a time. I could ask just one question, which needed only a yes or no, not requiring a difficult decision. If he became agitated, I needed to figure out what was wrong**

and speak soothingly. If I couldn't get him to understand me, I had to let it go and help him calm down with an easy jigsaw puzzle or a simple game he liked. Or best of all—music. Somehow music stimulates the memory. Tom could remember the words to old hymns and sing out happily. But above all, I had to never, never lose my patience. He couldn't help what was happening to him.

Yet as time went on, Jeri found it increasingly difficult to communicate with her husband. "Medication helped with the paranoia, but in just two years, Tom lost his ability to read, to write, and to converse intelligently. He didn't recognize our sons. He forgot bathing and bathroom skills. He wandered away if I let him out of my sight. I put alarms on the doors of our house so he couldn't get out in the middle of the night. Still, he got out once and the police had to search for him and bring him home."

One of the things that Jeri found helpful during these escapes was giving Tom a special bracelet. The bracelet had Jeri's name, phone number, and address, so searchers would be able to contact her in case Tom ever got lost again. These special bracelets can be used for

"Somehow music stimulates the memory. Tom could remember the words to old hymns and sing out happily. But above all, I had to never, never lose my patience. He couldn't help what was happening to him."

—Jeri Chase Ferris

other patients with Alzheimer's as well, and can be adapted so that a person can call a facility instead of the caregiver if the patient is in a memory care center or adult family home.

Three afternoons a week, Jeri took Tom to a day care center.

> **After he got over his fear at being left there, he began to love the coloring projects, the dance class, and singing old songs. There's something about music that must stay in a separate area of the brain—he always could sing the words to old favorites. When he wasn't at day care, Tom especially loved playing with our dog, car rides, and going to the store with me. And most of all, he loved going to the movies!**
>
> **One day Tom said he wanted to go to the movies, and he wanted to go now! I was really busy, but for some reason, I agreed. We saw a great movie about the racehorse Secretariat, then came home and had a glass of wine by the pool. It was a perfect day. And it was Tom's last day. He had a heart attack that night, and he died a few days later without ever waking up. I've often thought of that day. What if I had said, "I'm too busy. We'll go tomorrow"? I would have carried that guilt the rest of my life because there was no tomorrow.**

CHAPTER 7

Alzheimer's Disease Research

The first survivor of [Alzheimer's] is out there.
—*Alzheimer's Association*

An estimated 12.7 million Americans aged sixty-five and older may have Alzheimer's disease by 2050. Specialists in many fields are working together to discover better ways to treat Alzheimer's with the goal of one day learning how to prevent or even cure it. The US government has a national plan to prevent future cases of Alzheimer's and to meet the needs of the millions of people living with loved ones who have the disease. These goals include:

1. Preventing and effectively treating Alzheimer's
2. Enhancing the quality of care and improving efficiency
3. Supporting people with Alzheimer's and their families
4. Improving public awareness
5. Developing better data to track progress
6. Promoting healthy aging
7. Reducing risk factors for Alzheimer's

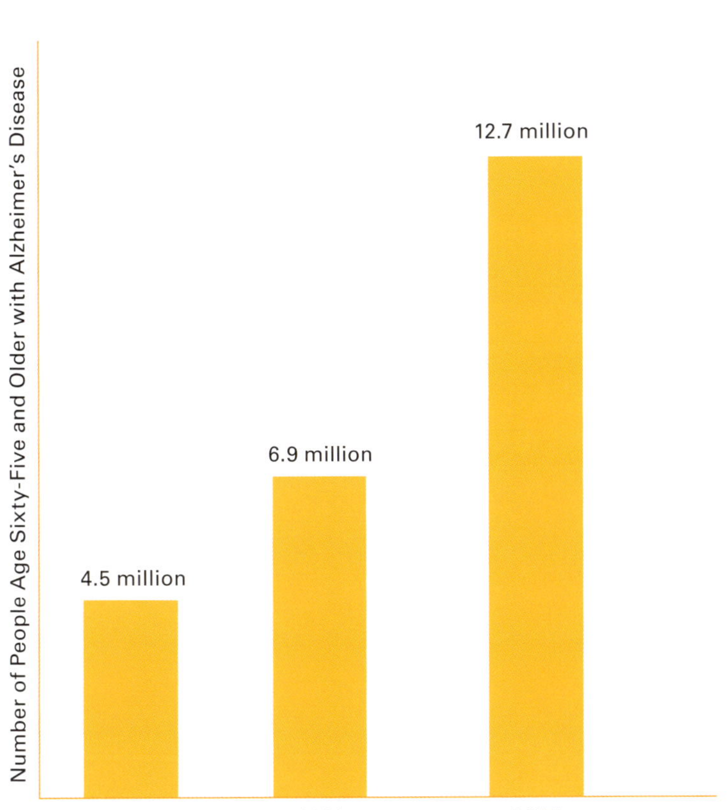

Sources: Liesi E. Hebert et. al, "Alzheimer Disease in the US Population: Prevalence Estimates Using the 2000 Census," *Archives of Neurology* 60 , no. 8 (August 2003): 1119–1122, doi:10.1001/archneur.60.8.1119; "Alzheimer's Disease Facts and Figures," Alzheimer's Association, Accessed June 20, 2024, https://www.alz.org/alzheimers-dementia/facts-figures.

In 2024 about 6.9 million Americans age sixty-five and older had Alzheimer's disease. By 2050 that number will likely reach 12.7 million.

Clinical Trials

Much of the work toward preventing and treating Alzheimer's disease takes place within clinical trials. Clinical trials are research studies that test new medications and treatments in people for many kinds of illnesses. Through these trials, researchers discover if a new medication or treatment is safe and effective. The trials are also designed to learn if a proposed new medication is more effective or has fewer harmful side effects than existing medications. Even before a clinical trial begins, scientists perform tests on the new medication in laboratories. If those studies are favorable, the FDA approves the proposed trial to be tested in people.

People volunteer to become part of clinical trials. Why would anyone volunteer to be what some may consider a human guinea pig? There are several reasons. Volunteers may want to contribute to discovering new information that could help themselves or others. Or perhaps the medication or treatment that some people are taking is not working very well, and they hope the new therapy will be more helpful. Many major medical breakthroughs could not happen without volunteers participating in clinical trials.

People who participate in clinical trials may receive either the medication or a placebo. The use of placebos is random and double-blinded, so neither the patient nor the researcher knows who receives the real medication and who receives the placebo. This ensures the results are accurate and unbiased. Until the trial is over, only the pharmacist who provides the medication knows if a patient is receiving the placebo or medication. Clinical trials have four phases:

PHASE 1

Is the medication safe? The medication is given for the first time to between twenty and one hundred people to determine its safety, dosage, and side effects. The participants may be healthy or may have the condition being studied. If those studies are favorable, the FDA approves the proposed medication to be tested in people. Phase 1 lasts several months.

PHASE 2

Does the medication work? If treatment in the smaller group seemed safe, a larger group of about three hundred people with the condition under study (for example, Alzheimer's) receive the medication to determine its effectiveness. Phase 2 lasts from a few months up to two years.

PHASE 3

How does the new medication compare with existing medications? At this stage, up to three thousand people with the condition under study take the medication to confirm its effectiveness, monitor side effects, and compare it with other medications that treat the same condition.

PHASE 4

This phase may involve thousands of people with the condition under study taking the medication for years to identify any long-term side effects and confirm its effectiveness.

While most clinical trials involve newly developed medications, other trials help researchers learn more about a disease or condition. For example, the BrainHealth Project is a ten-year study of one hundred thousand people to help identify factors that determine a healthy brain. The study contacts participants twice a year to perform online assessments to track their performance. Results may help researchers identify which behaviors, such as a balanced diet and routine exercise, may decrease the risk for developing Alzheimer's disease or another brain condition.

Studies in Progress

What are the benefits to people with Alzheimer's who enroll in clinical trials? The Alzheimer's Association points out several reasons to volunteer. Participants in a clinical trial can receive new medications or treatments before they're available to the general public. It lets people with early Alzheimer's have a more active role in their own health care. People in a clinical trial also receive expert care at major health-care facilities, often free of cost, as part of the study. Taking part in important medical research can be rewarding for many people. The US government funds more than five hundred clinical trials related to Alzheimer's disease, while other organizations and researchers are funding other studies. These trials investigate new medications and treatments, how to achieve an accurate diagnosis sooner, and techniques in caregiving.

MEDICATIONS

As of spring 2024, more than seventy clinical trials of medications for Alzheimer's were underway. Many of the medications target amyloid plaques and inflammation, while just two target tau tangles. A medication called donanemab completed Phase 3 trials in 2023 and was approved by the FDA in June 2024. The medication does not improve existing symptoms of Alzheimer's, but it can keep them from getting worse. Among people who started taking donanemab at the earliest stages of their disease, 47 percent had no disease progression after one year by some measurements, compared to 29 percent who took a placebo. The medication is much less effective among people with more advanced disease. A medication called ponesimod, used to treat multiple sclerosis, shows promise in mice with Alzheimer's. Ponesimod helps calm an overactive immune system, which is believed to be a component of Alzheimer's disease.

Another medication, Anavex 2-73, is an oral medication that reduces amyloid and inflammation when given to patients with mild cognitive impairment. The trial involved 509 people ages sixty to eighty-five. People who received Anavex had a 45 percent slower decline in their cognitive abilities compared to those receiving a placebo. Those people were also far more likely to experience significant improvement in overall function.

Mice with Alzheimer's Disease

While some people may disagree with using mice in experiments, researchers generally believe it to be ethical when an important potential benefit to human health cannot be obtained in another way. Scientists use mice with Alzheimer's disease to study how a medication or treatment might work in people. But Alzheimer's does not occur naturally in mice. Instead, scientists modify mouse genes, so the mice produce high levels of human amyloid in their brains. That means if something works well in mouse brains that have amyloid plaques, it might also work in humans who have Alzheimer's amyloid plaques.

VACCINES

A vaccine is a medication used to stimulate the body's immune system to fight a specific disease, often by injecting a weaker or inactive strain of the disease into the body. You've probably received vaccines for measles, mumps, chicken pox, and tetanus. Now researchers are testing vaccines to help prevent Alzheimer's disease. One of the clinical trial vaccines, UB-311, triggered helpful disease-fighting antibodies in 93 percent of patients with mild Alzheimer's. In people vaccinated with UB-311, the new antibodies significantly reduced amyloid, which could possibly slow or even prevent nerve damage. That in turn may slow or halt the progression of Alzheimer's. Another vaccine being tested in mice with Alzheimer's shows promise in reducing amyloid and decreasing brain inflammation.

Researchers are also looking into how the influenza vaccine, which is updated and administered every year, may affect the risk of Alzheimer's. They're finding some surprising results. People who received at least one flu shot over a four-year study were 40 percent less likely to develop Alzheimer's disease than people who did not receive a flu shot. Another study showed that people aged sixty-five and older who received common adult vaccinations against conditions such as tetanus and diptheria were 25 to 30 percent less likely to develop Alzheimer's than those who were unvaccinated.

DIAGNOSIS AND TREATMENT

The earlier a doctor can diagnose Alzheimer's disease in a patient, the greater the chance that medications and treatments can help prevent its progression. Many clinical trials research ways to get even earlier diagnoses. Researchers at Emory University found proteins in spinal fluid that can predict the possibility of Alzheimer's long before current tests can identify amyloid plaques and tau tangles.

In another clinical study, universities are investigating the use of a headband that generates small, controlled amounts of electricity to stimulate the brain. Patients with mild to moderate Alzheimer's wear the headband for fifteen minutes three times a day. The device has reduced inflammation caused by other conditions, and researchers hope it will do the same for people with Alzheimer's.

One company has developed a nasal spray medication. When tested in mice with Alzheimer's disease, the medication led to an improvement in symptoms even though the amount of amyloid did not decrease. Dr. Howard Weiner of Harvard Medical School said, "This represents a unique approach to treating Alzheimer's disease that could [possibly be used] in combination with anti-amyloid therapy."

GENE THERAPY

Researchers at Stanford University are experimenting with giving stem cells to mice with Alzheimer's disease. Stem cells are the building blocks for blood cells, brain cells, and most other cells in the body. The specialized stem cells used in the Stanford study reduced the amount of amyloid plaque in the mice. Meanwhile, researchers at the University of California, San Diego, have developed a method to genetically modify a protein that leads to amyloid in the brain. When the genetically modified protein is given to mice with Alzheimer's, it reduces both amyloid plaques and brain inflammation without harmful side effects. The results were promising enough that future studies are planned for human testing.

BOBI'S STORY: I Participate in Research Studies for Alzheimer's

Bobi Martin watched her sister-in-law, Mary Biedren, move through the advanced stages of Alzheimer's disease years ago. That experience made Bobi want to do something that might help prevent Alzheimer's in others. She enrolled in a study similar to the BrainHealth Project called the Brain Health Registry, which the University of California, San Francisco, and its partners manage. Its goal is to follow people over time, monitor their lifestyle and health practices, and see how those activities may affect the chance of developing Alzheimer's.

Bobi said, "It was heartbreaking to see my sister-in-law struggle to remember her family members. It was especially hard on her siblings and children when she began to hallucinate. Once I saw her touch her brother's hands and say, 'Oh these apples are getting soft. We need to throw them out.' Mary often 'saw' a little white dog that she would talk to and pet."

Mary's Alzheimer's helped Bobi learn how to communicate with someone with dementia. "Meet the person where they are," she said. "It isn't helpful to point out that they made a mistake, forgotten something you just said, or that someone they asked about died. It just confuses them and makes the person less likely to communicate."

Bobi enjoys participating in the study. She feels as if she's making a real contribution to the study of Alzheimer's disease. Every six months the organization sponsoring the study sends Bobi an email asking her to update her health history.

They ask me how many servings of fruit and vegetables I ate in the past two weeks, and how often I eat fish or red meat. There are questions about my exercise habits. Next,

Bobi Martin participates in a study to help researchers determine what behaviors may keep a person's brain in good health. Here, Bobi enjoys a healthful salad during a trip to Chile.

I take a series of timed memory tests online that involve remembering whether or not I've seen a particular image.

For example, there may be an image of a rowboat on a lake and a few minutes later there's a picture of a sailboat on a lake. I must answer whether or not I've seen that exact image before. Another test shows playing cards and asks if you saw the ten of hearts or the ten of diamonds. The tests get a bit more complicated as they progress. When I'm done, I must indicate how I think I did compared to others my age: better, average, or below average.

I joined this project because I wanted to do whatever I could do that might help with Alzheimer's research. Scientists need a large number of people in a study to see patterns that may contribute to a particular disease. The questions about how often I exercise, and whether I'm doing aerobics or strength training, can help researchers see how exercise affects my brain. The questions about how often I eat fruit, vegetables, and meat help them see if my diet is a contributing factor. It's crucial that I answer the questions honestly, rather than how I *think* I should respond because that could skew the data. I feel that helping scientists find a way to help stave off or prevent Alzheimer's is very important.

Bobi also thinks it's important for people to know about such studies and perhaps to participate in them, even if no one in their families has Alzheimer's.

"I joined this project because I wanted to do whatever I could do that might help with Alzheimer's research. Scientists need a large number of people in a study to see patterns that may contribute to a particular disease. The questions about how often I exercise, and whether I'm doing aerobics or strength training, can help researchers see how exercise affects my brain."

—*Bobi Martin*

What Can I Do?

Now that you know more about Alzheimer's disease, you may wonder how you can help. You can do a lot by helping to raise awareness of Alzheimer's. Many cities hold an annual Walk to End Alzheimer's event. You could join a planned walk or organize one just for teens. Young people can encourage their high schools to invite an expert on Alzheimer's disease to talk with the student body. If you have a writing assignment, you can write a paper about Alzheimer's and include interviews from experts (and maybe a patient) in it. Students looking for community service projects to include on college applications could visit a facility with Alzheimer's patients and spend time with the staff and learn how to interact with patients. Hold a neighborhood bake sale on your street or at a community center, and donate the proceeds to your local Alzheimer's organization.

Walk to End Alzheimer's is one of the largest fundraising events for Alzheimer's care, support, and research, and takes place in hundreds of cities each year. Participants may walk holding flowers. Purple is for those who have lost someone to Alzheimer's, yellow is for caregivers, and orange is for supporters.

If you know somebody or have a loved one with Alzheimer's, the Alzheimer's Association website lists fifty activities that you can do together. These include outdoor activities, such as planting flowers and feeding the birds; indoor activities, such as playing checkers and looking at family photographs and magazines together; something personal, such as brushing hair and applying hand lotion; something in the kitchen, such as setting the table and making lunch together; and celebrating family traditions, such as baking holiday desserts and decorating a tree.

Music can be a rewarding activity as well. Sing together and listen to the patient's favorite songs. According to the Alzheimer's Association, "Music can be powerful. Studies have shown music may reduce agitation and improve behavioral issues that are common in the middle stages of the disease. Even in the late stages of Alzheimer's, a person may be able to tap a beat or sing lyrics to a song from childhood. Music provides a way to connect, even after verbal communication has become difficult."

Alzheimer's can be a frightening disease. Yet family and friends can help make it more bearable by learning about it, visiting their loved ones as often as possible, and adapting their communication skills as needed. Because Alzheimer's is so prevalent—and likely to become much more so as the population ages—researchers are looking for ways to diagnose Alzheimer's earlier, better ways to treat it and, hopefully, ways to prevent it entirely. While these discoveries may not benefit a person who has advanced Alzheimer's now, new medications and treatments are already helping some Alzheimer's patients. Scientists around the world are working hard to ensure that even more preventive measures, medications, and treatments are on the way.

Glossary

Alzheimer's disease: the most common form of dementia, caused by the buildup of abnormal proteins in the brain. It results in severe damage to brain cells, which ultimately causes the loss of most normal functions and leads to death.

amyloid plaques: formed by sticky pieces of the protein beta-amyloid that clump together and build up in the spaces between brain cells, hindering communication between the cells

cerebrospinal fluid (CSF): the fluid that surrounds and protects the brain and spinal cord

clinical trial: a formal research study that tests a new medication or other treatment in people. Clinical trials are the primary way that researchers discover if a new medication, treatment, or medical device is safe and effective in people.

cognition: mental processes that take place in the brain, including thinking, learning, memory, and perception

dementia: a range of medical conditions that lead to a decline in thinking, reasoning, and memory

early-onset Alzheimer's: Alzheimer's that develops before the age of sixty-five. It is often linked to a genetic defect.

frontotemporal dementia (FTD): a type of dementia that mainly affects the frontal and temporal lobes of the brain, often causing dramatic changes in personality or loss of language skills

Lewy body dementia (DLB): a type of dementia similar to Alzheimer's caused by large deposits of Lewy body proteins in the brain that results in a decline in thinking, reasoning, hallucinations, and problems with movement

Mini-Cog test: a test that assesses a person's cognition and memory, which is used to determine if further testing is needed to rule if Alzheimer's is present

PET scan: short for *positron emission tomography scan*. It uses a radioactive substance to detect amyloid plaques and tau tangles in the brain.

tau tangles: twisted fibers of a protein called tau that gather inside brain cells and prevent the normal transport of vital nutrients to the brain

vascular dementia: a type of dementia caused by decreased blood flow to the brain, such as from a stroke. Symptoms depend on what part of the brain is affected.

Source Notes

4 "Our vision . . . all other dementia.": "FY23-FY25 Strategic Plan," Alzheimer's Association, accessed April 8, 2024, https://www.alz.org/media/Documents/strategic-plan-fy2023-fy2025.pdf.

4–5 "My parents both . . . part of my life.": Maralyn Soifer, interview with the author, March 14, 2023.

9 "a syndrome . . . biological ageing.": "Dementia," World Health Organization, March 15, 2023, https://www.who.int/news-room/fact-sheets/detail/dementia.

11–13 "It was ten days . . . family home.": Kevan Atteberry, interview with the author, September 4, 2023.

13 "It took white . . . whole life, smiling.": Atteberry.

14 "Alzheimer's disease and dementia . . . fight Alzheimer's disease.": "12 Myths about Alzheimer's Disease," National Institute on Aging, accessed April 8, 2024, https://www.nia.nih.gov/health/alzheimers-and-dementia/12-myths-about-alzheimers-disease.

16 "For years . . . away from me.": Margarita Engle, interview with the author, May 22, 2023.

16–17 "I realized . . . gentle expectations." Engle.

18 "If I get dementia . . . family gatherings.": Rachael Wonderlin, *When Someone You Know Is Living in a Dementia Care Community: Words to Say and Things to Do* (Baltimore: John Hopkins University Press, 2016), xi.

19 "Normal brain aging . . . improve with age.": "Recognizing Symptoms of Dementia and Seeking Help," Centers for Disease Control and Prevention, accessed April 8, 2024, https://www.cdc.gov/aging/publications/features/dementia-not-normal-aging.html.

20 "a peculiar . . . cerebral cortex.": Alois Alzheimer, quoted in Hanns Hippius and Gabriele Neundörfer, "The Discovery of Alzheimer's Disease," *Dialogues in Clinical Neuroscience* 5, no. 1 (March 5, 2003): 101–108, https://doi.org/10.31887/DCNS.2003.5.1/hhippius.

22 "My main goal . . . especially African Americans.": David Ajibade, quoted in Breana Ross, "'It's Tearing Families Apart': Doctor Aims to Reduce Impact of Alzheimer's on Black Communities," WBAL-TV 11, updated June 26, 2023, https://www.wbaltv.com/article/alzheimers-disease-black-communities-dr-david-ajibade/44345161.

24 "Words cannot convey . . . they were doing.": Patty Gregory, interview with the author, June 1, 2023.

24–25 “Barbara was never . . . with her brain.”: Gregory.

25 “I’ll always remember . . . she died.”: Gregory.

25 “Your family is going . . . another person.”: Gregory.

26 “Never too early, never too late.”: “World Alzheimer’s Month,” Alzheimer’s Disease International, accessed April 16, 2024, https://www.alzint.org/get-involved/world-alzheimers-month/.

29 “At first, my mom and I . . . do about it.”: Mark Zanzinger, interview with the author, May 9, 2023.

29 “You’ve got to . . . can do.”: Zanzinger.

29–30 “He’s made friends . . . active every day.”: Zanzinger.

30 “Something that I didn’t . . . most weekends.”: Zanzinger.

30–31 “When something this big . . . you feel good.”: Zanzinger.

33 “If I get dementia . . . want to be treated.”: Wonderlin, *When Someone You Know*, xi.

33–34 “Most Alzheimer’s dementia patients . . . person to person.”: Wessam Labib, quoted in Molly Smith, “Catching Alzheimer’s Early: Signs to Look for in a Loved One,” Loma Linda University Health, June 27, 2023, https://news.llu.edu/health-wellness/catching-alzheimer-s-early-signs-look-for-loved-one.

39 “My mom was sixty-three . . . journey ahead.“: Michele Langhorst, interview with the author, May 5, 2023.

40 “The hardest part . . . I cling to.”: Langhorst.

40 “We first put Mom . . . best outcome.”: Langhorst.

41 “Mom would have wanted . . . found love again.”: Langhorst.

41 “Don’t be upset . . . “time goes on.”: Langhorst.

41 “I held Mom’s hand . . . she wanted to do.”: Langhorst.

41 “Mom came to me . . . she’s at peace.”: Langhorst.

42–43 “Be open and direct . . . support and research.”: “Overcoming Stigma,” Alzheimer’s Association, accessed April 8, 2024, https://www.alz.org/help-support/i-have-alz/overcoming-stigma.

45 “This study . . . Alzheimer’s brains.”: C. Kathleen Dorey, quoted in Virginia Tech, “Eat Your Vegetables to Protect Your Brain,” EurekAlert!, August 14, 2023, https://www.eurekalert.org/news-releases/998575.

47 “The day with . . . activity of their choice.”: “Go Purple to Raise Awareness for Alzheimer’s,” Alzheimer’s Association, accessed April 8, 2024, https://www.alz.org/abam/overview.asp.

48 "If I get dementia . . . you know and love.": Wonderlin, *When Someone You Know*, xi.

49–50 "Problems with judgment . . . problems with thinking and/or memory?": AD8 Dementia Screening Interview, Alzheimer's Association, accessed April 8, 2024, https://www.alz.org/media/documents/ad8-dementia-screening.pdf.

56 "Blood tests for . . . more widely available.": Sebastian Palmqvist, quoted in "Simple Finger Prick Test Exemplifies Advances in Alzheimer's Disease Blood Tests," Alzheimer's Association, International Conference, July 19, 2023, https://aaic.alz.org/releases_2023/finger-prick-blood-test-alzheimers-disease.asp.

56 "It's something that five years . . . in the blood.": Gil Rabinovici, quoted in Brenda Goodman, "With New Therapies That Promise to Slow Alzheimer's Disease, Researchers Race to Reform How Patients Are Diagnosed," CNN, July 16, 2023, https://www.cnn.com/2023/07/16/health/race-to-reform-alzheimers-disease-diagnosis.

56 "early memory . . . uncertain cause.": Rabinovici.

57 "At first . . . in the future.": Bobbie Brubaker, interview with the author, May 15, 2023.

57–58 "David developed prostate cancer . . . San Francisco.": Brubaker.

58–59 "We lived through . . . almost anything.": Brubaker.

59 "The Mini-Cog . . . thorough evaluation.": Soo Borson, interview with the author, June 25, 2023.

60 "Maybe mine are lost . . . not ever / ever.": Eugenia Zukerman, poem from *Like Falling through a Cloud: A Lyrical Memoir of Coping with Forgetfulness, Confusion, and a Dreaded Diagnosis* (Bridgehampton, NY: East End, 2019), 4.

61 "This treatment . . . hobbies and interests.": Joanne Pike, quoted in "Alzheimer's Association Welcomes U.S. FDA Traditional Approval of Leqembi," Alzheimer's Association, July 6, 2023, https://www.alz.org/news/2023/lecanemab-leqembi-traditional-fda-approval.

61 "due to the serious side effects . . . as long as necessary.": "Dementia-Related Behaviors," Alzheimer's Association, accessed April 8, 2024, https://www.alz.org/media/Documents/alzheimers-dementia-related-behaviors-ts.pdf.

62 "When my mom . . . hardest on them.": Carlie Sokol, interview with the author, June 5, 2023.

63 "If someone you love . . . favorite memories of them.": Sokol.

64 "In ongoing clinical trials . . . disease and diabetes.": "Treatment," Alzheimer's Los Angeles, accessed April 8, 2024, https://www.alzheimersla.org/for-families/understanding-memory-loss/treatment/.

64 "Provide time for . . . difficult emotions.": "Accepting the Diagnosis," Alzheimer's Association, accessed April 8, 2024, https://www.alz.org/help-support/caregiving/stages-behaviors/accepting_the_diagnosis.

65 "If I get dementia . . . visit me often.": Wonderlin, *When Someone You Know*, xi.

68 "Every day I make . . . from their own lives.": Abaigeal Johnson, interview with the author, June 5, 2023.

68 "Activity programs should . . . and accomplishment.": Johnson.

68 "My favorite question . . . keep on going.": Johnson.

71 "Store potentially . . . doors are visible.": "Home Safety Checklist," Alzheimer's Association, accessed April 8, 2024, https://alz.org/media/Documents/alzheimers-dementia-home-safety-checklist.pdf.

74 "Before my grandma . . . eventually progress.": Charlie Poole, interview with the author, April 17, 2023.

75–77 "Both of our parents . . . than it is currently.": Poole.

76 "I'll never forget . . . and did laundry.": Sara Poole, interview with the author, April 17, 2023.

77–78 "Whenever I talk about . . . others feel the same.": Charlie Poole, interview.

78 "One of the main reasons . . . I am unapologetic.": Sara Poole, interview with the author, July 24, 2023.

79 "In today's modern society . . . put others first.": Connie Siskowski and Keisha L. Jackson, "American Association of Caregiving Youth Supports Young Unsung Heroes," Crusader Newspaper Group, September 9, 2021, https://chicagocrusader.com/american-association-of-caregiving-youth-supports-young-unsung-heroes/.

79–80 "We helped care . . . understands like caregivers.": "About," Kids Are Caregivers Too, accessed April 8, 2024, https://www.kidsarecaregiverstoo.com/about-us.html.

81 "She loved cookies . . . who we were.": "A Kid Crisis in the United States," Kids Are Caregivers Too, accessed April 8, 2024, https://www.kidsarecaregiverstoo.com/goals.html.

81 "Caregivers must focus . . . caregiving journey.": Family Caregiver Alliance, reviewed by Bruce R. Reed, "Alzheimer's Disease and Caregiving," Family Caregiver Alliance, accessed April 8, 2024, https://www.caregiver.org/resource/alzheimers-disease-caregiving/.

82 "If I get dementia . . . that I am.": Wonderlin, *When Someone You Know*, x.

85 "joined forced to engage . . . inspire change.": "The Youth Movement against Alzheimer's," Hilarity for Charity, accessed April 8, 2024, https://www.wearehfc.org/ymaa.

86 "I'd only been . . . take action.": Hamza Najjar, interview with the author, August 4, 2023.

86–87 "I made this a top priority . . . becomes worth it.": Najjar.

88 "Monday through Thursday . . . for others.": Najjar.

88 "It's much harder . . . all worthwhile.": Najjar.

89 "Talk about . . . 'Don't you remember?'": Atteberry, interview.

89 "Limit giving . . . is important.": Brubaker, interview.

90 "Never argue . . . cheerful subject.": Engle, interview.

90 "Meet the person . . . enter yours.": Gregory, interview.

90 "Know what stage . . . ways to communicate.": Langhorst, interview.

90 "Whatever you need . . . they're people too.": Najjar, interview.

90 "Patience is the most . . . mental health.": Charlie Poole, interview.

90 "Spend time with . . . shine through.": Sokol, interview.

90 "Be prepared . . . got to be patient.": Zanzinger, interview.

91 "As a physician . . . little white lies.": Sandeep Jauhar, quoted in Bridget Balch, "Facing Alzheimer's as a Physician and Caregiver," AAMC, August 3, 2023, https://www.aamc.org/news/facing-alzheimer-s-physician-and-caregiver.

92 "I was ten years old . . . I'd help.": Kaylin Jean-Louis, interview with the author, May 8, 2023.

92 "Although her conversations . . . greater than dementia.": "About Priscilla," Priscilla Jean-Louis, accessed April 8, 2024, https://www.priscillajjean-louis.com/.

92–93 "My responsibilities as the secondary . . . journey easier.": Kaylin Jean-Louis, interview.

93–94 "It can be . . . the situation.": Jean-Louis.

94 "Today, we make . . . greater than dementia.": Kaylin's Caring Konnection, Facebook, September 21, 2023, https://www.facebook.com/kaylinscaringkonnection.

94–95 “My grandmother brings me joy . . . like before.”: Kaylin Jean-Louis, interview.

95 “While there were . . . anything in the world.”: Jean-Louis.

95 “I want to encourage . . . to get advice.”: Jean-Louis.

97 “My husband, Tom . . . doctor for a checkup.”: Jeri Chase Ferris, interview with the author, July 10, 2023.

97–98 “I found new ways . . . happening to him.”: Ferris.

98 “Medication helped . . . bring him home.”: Ferris.

99 “After he got over . . . there was no tomorrow.”: Ferris.

100 “The first survivor . . . out there.”: “The First Survivor of Alzheimer’s Is Out There, but We Won’t Get There without You,” Alzheimer’s Association, accessed April 8, 2024, https://www.alz.org/about/awareness-initiatives/first-survivor.

106 “This represents . . . anti-amyloid therapy.”: Howard Weiner, quoted in “Study Evaluating Intranasal Anti-CD3 for Treatment of Alzheimer’s Disease Published in the *PNAS Journal*,” News Medical Life Sciences, September 9, 2023, https://www.news-medical.net/news/20230909/Study-evaluating-intranasal-anti-CD3-for-treatment-of-Alzheimere28099s-disease-published-in-the-PNAS-journal.aspx.

107 “It was heartbreaking . . . talk to and pet.”: Bobi Martin, interviews with the author, February 27, 2023; April 30, 2023; July 2, 2023.

107 “Meet the person . . . likely to communicate.”: Martin.

107–109 “They ask me how . . . is very important.”: Martin.

111 “Music can be powerful . . . has become difficult.”: “Art and Music,” Alzheimer’s Association, accessed April 8, 2024, https://www.alz.org/help-support/caregiving/daily-care/art-music.

Selected Bibliography

"Alzheimer's Disease and Related Dementias." Centers for Disease Control and Prevention. Accessed April 2, 2024. https://www.cdc.gov/aging/aginginfo/alzheimers.htm.

"Alzheimer's Disease Facts and Figures." Alzheimer's Association. Accessed April 2, 2024. https://www.alz.org/alzheimers-dementia/facts-figures.

Bridges, Khiara M. "Implicit Bias and Racial Disparities in Health Care." American Bar Association. Accessed April 2, 2024. https://www.americanbar.org/groups/crsj/publications/human_rights_magazine_home/the-state-of-healthcare-in-the-united-states/racial-disparities-in-health-care/.

"Caregiving." Alzheimer's Association. Accessed April 2, 2024. https://www.alz.org/help-support/caregiving.

"Clinical Trials." Mayo Clinic. Accessed April 2, 2024. https://www.mayo.edu/research/clinical-trials/diseases-conditions/alzheimer%27s-disease/.

"NIA-Funded Active Alzheimer's and Related Dementias Clinical Trials and Studies." National Institute on Aging. Accessed April 2, 2024. https://www.nia.nih.gov/research/ongoing-AD-trials.

"Overcoming Stigma." Alzheimer's Association. Accessed April 2, 2024. https://www.alz.org/help-support/i-have-alz/overcoming-stigma.

"Research and Progress." Alzheimer's Association. Accessed April 2, 2024. https://www.alz.org/alzheimers-dementia/research_progress.

"Risk Factors and Risk Reduction." Alzheimer's Disease International. Accessed April 2, 2024. https://www.alzint.org/about/risk-factors-risk-reduction/.

Siskowski, Connie, and Keisha L. Jackson. "American Association of Caregiving Youth Supports Young Unsung Heroes." American Association of Caregiving Youth, September 9, 2021. https://aacy.org/american-association-of-caregiving-youth-supports-young-unsung-heroes/.

Smith, Molly. "Catching Alzheimer's Early: Signs to Look for in a Loved One." Loma Linda University Health, June 27, 2023. https://news.llu.edu/health-wellness/catching-alzheimer-s-early-signs-look-for-loved-one.

"Stages of Alzheimer's." Alzheimer's Association. Accessed April 2, 2024. https://www.alz.org/alzheimers-dementia/stages.

"10 Early Signs and Symptoms of Alzheimer's and Dementia." Alzheimer's Association. Accessed April 2, 2024. https://www.alz.org/alzheimers-dementia/10_signs.

"Treatments for Alzheimer's." Alzheimer's Association. Accessed April 2, 2024. https://www.alz.org/alzheimers-dementia/treatments.

"What Are the Signs of Alzheimer's Disease?" National Institute on Aging. Accessed April 2, 2024. https://www.nia.nih.gov/health/alzheimers-symptoms-and-diagnosis/what-are-signs-alzheimers-disease.

"What Causes Alzheimer's Disease?" National Institute on Aging. Accessed April 2, 2024. https://www.nia.nih.gov/health/alzheimers-causes-and-risk-factors/what-causes-alzheimers-disease.

"What Happens to the Brain in Alzheimer's Disease?" National Institute on Aging. Accessed April 2, 2024. https://www.nia.nih.gov/health/alzheimers-causes-and-risk-factors/what-happens-brain-alzheimers-disease.

"What Is Dementia?" Alzheimer's Association. Accessed April 2, 2024. https://www.alz.org/alzheimers-dementia/what-is-dementia.

Wonderlin, Rachael. *When Someone You Know Is Living in a Dementia Care Community.* Baltimore: Johns Hopkins University Press, 2016.

Further Information

BOOKS

Budson, Andrew E., and Maureen K. O'Connor. *Six Steps to Managing Alzheimer's Disease and Dementia: A Guide for Families*. New York: Oxford University Press, 2021.
Caregiver needs are just as important as the needs of a loved one or family member with Alzheimer's disease. Learn more about caregiving in an easy-to-read style that features vignettes and stories with real-life examples of how to successfully manage these conditions.

Engle, Margarita. *Eloísa's Musical Window*. New York: Atheneum Books for Young Readers, 2024.
This story is a tribute to Engle's mother, Eloisa, who has Alzheimer's disease and is featured in chapter 1 of this book. As a child in Cuba, Eloisa's family couldn't afford a radio, so she sat by a window and listened to music coming from her neighbor's house. Then musicians began practicing on the street in front of Eloisa's house, and soon the window became a musical portal to joy.

Goldsmith, Connie. *Smashing Stigma: Dismantling Stereotypes, Prejudice, and Discrimination*. Minneapolis: Twenty-First Century Books, 2024.
Stigma leads to harmful stereotypes, prejudice, and discrimination. It can keep people from seeking the help and support they need. They may internalize others' stigma and start to blame themselves for their condition or experiences. Sometimes the effects of stigma can even be life-threatening. Learn how to recognize and battle stigma and its devastating effects.

Graff-Radford, Jonathan, and Angela M. Lunde. *Mayo Clinic on Alzheimer's Disease and Other Dementias*. Rochester, MN: Mayo Clinic, 2020.
This book discusses the latest research on the prevention and treatment of Alzheimer's and other dementias, and offers advice for living with it. Discover tips for managing the daily challenge of caring for someone with dementia and how to tell the difference between the normal signs of aging and dementia.

Johns Hopkins editors. *The Science of Alzheimer's*. Baltimore: Johns Hopkins University Press, 2023.
This book offers advice on how to work with Alzheimer's patients, guiding readers toward acceptance and compassion, and using humor to cope.

Mace, Nancy L., and Peter V. Rabins. *The 36-Hour Day: A Family Guide to Caring for People Who Have Alzheimer Disease and Other Dementias.* Baltimore: Johns Hopkins University Press, 2021.
Learn about Alzheimer's and dementia, its causes, how to manage its early stages, and caregiving during Alzheimer's later stage.

Ricardi, Sharon. *The Future of Alzheimer's: Finding Inspiration & Hope through Expert Insight.* Hobart, NY: Hatherleigh, 2024.
This book quotes twenty experts on Alzheimer's disease. All experts offer advice to people with loved ones who are newly diagnosed with Alzheimer's, and they answer whether there will ever be a cure for the disease.

WEBSITES AND ORGANIZATIONS

Alzheimer's Association
https://www.alz.org/
The Alzheimer's Association is a leader in the drive to end Alzheimer's. It promotes global research and early detection. The organization provides information on everything about Alzheimer's, from symptoms, diagnosis, caregiving, communication, research, and more.

Alzheimer's Disease International
https://www.alzint.org/resource/world-alzheimer-report-2023/
This group partners with the World Health Organization. It works with Alzheimer associations in more than 120 countries, as well as with patients and caregivers. You can download its *World Alzheimer Report* to examine factors in many countries that contribute to or seem to decrease the risk of developing Alzheimer's.

Hilarity for Charity
https://www.wearehfc.org/
This is a national nonprofit organization that works with families impacted by Alzheimer's disease. It focuses on helping caregivers and offers links to programs and workshops.

Kids Are Caregivers Too
https://www.kidsarecaregiverstoo.com/
More than five million kids in the United States live with and help provide daily care for household members with Alzheimer's and other medical and mental conditions. The site talks about the challenges and opportunities of youth caregiving from the point of view of young people who have done this. It discusses subjects not normally covered by other

Alzheimer's sites, including ways that young caregivers can connect online for understanding and support.

Mayo Clinic
https://www.mayoclinic.org/diseases-conditions/alzheimers-disease/symptoms-causes/syc-20350447
The Mayo Clinic is a recognized national leader in both providing health care and educating the public about it. The clinic is well known for providing expert information about many diseases and conditions, including Alzheimer's. This is a good site to review for someone with limited time, as it thoroughly covers Alzheimer's basics.

National Institute on Aging
https://www.nia.nih.gov/health/topics/alzheimers-and-dementia
This site helps readers learn more about Alzheimer's disease and its diagnosis and treatment. It provides tips and resources for caregivers. In addition to covering Alzheimer's and other dementias, the site discusses healthy lifestyles including diets, dispels common myths, and details early-onset Alzheimer's.

World Health Organization
https://www.who.int/news-room/fact-sheets/detail/dementia
The World Health Organization is the United Nations agency responsible for international public health. Its section about Alzheimer's disease provides excellent information about the following: key facts, overview, common kinds of dementia, symptoms, treatment and care, and risk factors and prevention.

AUDIO, MOVIES, AND VIDEOS

Alzheimer's Association. YouTube Channel. https://www.youtube.com/user/actionalz.
This YouTube channel offers an authoritative collection of videos that span many aspects of Alzheimer's disease. Subjects include risk reduction, maintaining independence, new treatments, advancing equity of medical care for Alzheimer's, highlights of the most recent annual convention, and more.

"Alzheimer's Disease—Plaques, Tangles, Causes, Symptoms & Pathology." YouTube video, 8:53. Posted by Osmosis from Elsevier, March 22, 2016. https://www.youtube.com/watch?v=v5gdH_Hydes.
This is an animated video that covers the plaques and tangles found in Alzheimer's in a way that makes these complex findings easier to understand.

"Alzheimer's Podcasts." Centers for Disease Control and Prevention. https://www.cdc.gov/aging/publications/podcasts.htm.
This site offers more than twenty audio podcasts on a wide variety of topics related to Alzheimer's disease, making it an excellent source for family research.

"ALZ Talks: Dementia and the Whole Family." YouTube video, 28:26. Posted by Alzheimer's Association, June 27, 2022. https://youtu.be/kvxJrfAvAjk.6.
Kaylin and Priscilla Jean-Louis recorded this Zoom presentation in association with the Alzheimer's Association. This mother-daughter caregiving team share their perspectives on navigating the condition, and how they support each other and other caregivers.

Call the Doctor. "All about Alzheimer's Disease." Video, 25:00. Public Broadcasting Service, March 16, 2022. https://www.pbs.org/video/all-about-alzheimers-disease-fvkqqm/.
A panel of experts presents a broad view of the causes, symptoms, treatment, and caregiving involved with Alzheimer's disease. The video stresses the importance of early diagnosis.

"Healthy Aging: Promoting Well-Being in Older Adults." YouTube video, 1:05:04. Centers for Disease Control and Prevention (CDC), September 22, 2017. https://www.youtube.com/watch?v=Zdfw8uQ-vA4.
This is an excellent video about all aspects of health for older people and how better health may decrease the risk of Alzheimer's disease.

Hill, Carrie. "15 Movies about Dementia and Alzheimer's." verywell health, July 10, 2023. https://www.verywellhealth.com/movies-about-dementia-and-alzheimers-disease-97664.
The site lists fifteen movies about Alzheimer's and other dementias, all approved by experts. Topics range from caregiving to end-of-life themes. Search the list of movies for one that fits with your situation or what you'd like to learn more about.

"Kids Are Caregivers Too | Alzheimer's Caregiving Speech | Brain Bowl 2020 | Boca Raton, Florida." YouTube video, 14:47. Posted by A Little bit of Happy, February 1, 2020. https://www.youtube.com/watch?v=qn3_opMKpOM.
Brothers Charlie and AJ Poole give an excellent presentation about their caregiving experience for their grandmother who had Alzheimer's.

“Protecting Yourself from Alzheimer’s Disease.” YouTube video, 3:13. Posted by CBS Pittsburgh, September 7, 2023. https://www.youtube.com/watch?v=06Nu2vmxIiY.

This news special was presented to mark Alzheimer’s Awareness Month with easy-to-understand information about what people can do when they’re young to decrease the risk of Alzheimer’s.

“Understanding Alzheimer’s Disease.” Video, 2:02. Oregon Science and Health University. Accessed April 2, 2024. https://www.ohsu.edu/brain-institute/understanding-alzheimers-disease.

This easy-to-watch video covers the basics of Alzheimer’s disease, including an overview of the disease, its causes, symptoms, and treatment. It closes by recommending that family members work with health-care providers to develop a plan that is right for the patient.

Index

About the Author

Connie Goldsmith has written nearly thirty nonfiction books. Her books for young adult and middle-grade readers include subjects such as health topics, history, and military themes. She has also published more than two hundred magazine articles for adults and children. Her most recent books are *Pigeons at War: How Avian Heroes Changed History*; *Smashing Stigma: Dismantling Stereotypes, Prejudice, and Discrimination*; *Running on Empty: Sleeplessness in American Teens*; *Kiyo Sato: From a WWII Japanese Internment Camp to a Life of Service* (a Eureka Gold medal recipient); *Pandemic: How Climate, the Environment, and Superbugs Increase the Risk*; and *Bombs Over Bikini: The World's First Nuclear Disaster*, a Junior Library Guild Selection, Children's Book Committee/Bank Street College Best Children's Book of Year, and SCBWI Crystal Kite winner.

Goldsmith is a longtime member of the Society of Children's Book Writers and Illustrators, and the Authors Guild. She is a registered nurse with a bachelor of science degree in nursing and a master of public administration degree in health care. She lives near Sacramento, California.

Photo Acknowledgments

Image credits: Anna Bergbauer/Getty Images, p. 6; Vitalii Petrenko/Shutterstock, p. 7; Courtesy of Kevan Atteberry, p. 11; Courtesy of Margarita Engle, p. 17; IanDagnall Computing/Alamy, p. 20; San Francisco Chronicle/Hearst Newspapers/Getty Images, p. 21; Courtesy of Terra Prestwich, p. 25; AP Photo/Sarah A. Miller, p. 26; Courtesy of Rita Zanzinger, p. 31; elenabs/Getty Images, p. 36; AP Photo/United States Postal Service, p. 38; Courtesy of Michele Langhorst and Lance L. Langhorst, p. 39; william87/Getty Images, p. 45; ZUMA Press Inc/Alamy, p. 47; Reprinted with permission from Dr. Soo Borson, pp. 51–52; inspiring.team/Shutterstock, p. 53; Alila Medical Media/Shutterstock, p. 54; Courtesy of Barbara Brubaker, p. 58; Courtesy of Linda Kosut Lyon, p. 63; Courtesy of Denise Reason, p. 68; National Institutes of Health/Department of Health and Human Services, p. 70; Courtesy of Sara Poole, pp. 76, 80; Rick Kern/Stringer/Getty Images, p. 85; Courtesy of Sami Najjar, p. 87; Courtesy of Priscilla Jean-Louis, p. 93; NurPhoto/Getty Images, p. 96; Courtesy of Kim Ellis, p. 108; AP Photo/Austen Leake, p. 110. Design element: D things/Shutterstock.
Cover: D things/Shutterstock. Back cover: Jolygon/Shutterstock.